How to be a Successful

Also available from Continuum

How to Run Your School Successfully, Adrian Percival and
   Susan Tranter
How to Run Your Department Successfully, Chris Turner
How to be a Successful Deputy Head, Geoff Brookes
How to be a Successful Form Tutor, Michael Marland CBE and
   Rick Rogers

How to be a Successful Head of Year

A Practical Guide

Brian Carline

continuum

Continuum International Publishing Group

The Tower Building	80 Maiden Lane
11 York Road	Suite 704
London	New York
SE1 7NX	NY 10038

www.continuumbooks.com

British Library Cataloguing-in-Publication Data
A catalogue record for this book is available from the British Library.

ISBN: 0–8264–9644–X (paperback)

Library of Congress Cataloging-in-Publication Data
A catalog record for this book is available from the Library of Congress.

Typeset by RefineCatch Limited, Bungay, Suffolk
Printed and bound in Great Britain by Ashford Colour Press, Gosport, Hampshire

For Nancy and Betty

Contents

Acknowledgements

I would like to thank Derek Fawbert, Graham Griffiths, David Morley and Rob Woodburn for their help with recalling some of the amusing anecdotes in this book. My special thanks go to all the heads of year with whom I have worked, whose enthusiasm and assiduous nature inspired me to write this book.

Introduction

Some years ago I had the misfortune to work with a teaching colleague who showed all the charm and bonhomie of Josef Mengele. I was reminded of an expression frequently used by my uncle Horace, suitably describing the nature of this member of the teaching fraternity.

'I'll tell thee lad,' he would sagaciously recall, 'he's the kind of bloke who'd wee on your back and tell you that you were sweating!'

The urinating gentleman in question was a main-scale teacher whose attempts to go through the performance threshold appeared about as straightforward as trying to plait sawdust. Along with a distinct lack of people skills, he was indolent and all for an easy life.

It came as quite a shock to us all when one day he announced to everyone that he'd secured a new job as head of year at a secondary school in the inner city.

'Head of Year 8!' he bellowed across a busy staffroom. 'Yeah, that's me! Plenty of hankies to wipe noses. Give 'em a bollocking every now and then. Get me tutors to do all the work. Sorted!' This was his rather unique and deluded interpretation of his new job description.

There was a noticeable lack of tears and sadness shown by

his colleagues at the end of term as our pastoral guru left to take up his new and peaceful position. Indeed, there was probably more sorrow shown for John Prescott when his hanky-panky caused him to journey through troubled domestic times.

Any person who subscribes to the above pastoral formula of an effortless life, and is contemplating applying for a similar post of responsibility, must on no account post the letter. However, anyone who is currently a pastoral middle manager and supports this fallacious prescription for job success, should instantly pen a letter. On this occasion, it should be a letter of resignation and make sure you post it this time!

At the risk of being castigated, or even castrated by heads of department, I view head of year as the hardest position in the middle management of secondary schools. Year heads constitute the engine room of a school. They allow schools to tick over on a daily basis. They are people who are on call from the moment they enter the school building until the time they leave. In the course of a typical school week, you, as year manager will wear many hats. You will feel comfortable in some while others you will slowly grow into. You will be doctor, disciplinarian and detective one day, you will be arbitrator, motivator and facilitator the next.

The post of head of year has undergone a necessary important metamorphosis over the last 30 years. Schools have increased in population size and they must be divided into manageable sections to oversee and cater for the individual needs of students. The head of year fulfils this need. The job has grown with time. As the demands placed upon classroom teachers have increased, so too has the job description for heads of year. The job is open to all teachers from all subject backgrounds. It is no longer the prerogative and sole licence of PE staff.

The job is exhausting. The job often goes with you when you are at home. You will feel there aren't enough hours in the school day for you to shoulder your workload. However, it is one of the most rewarding and satisfying jobs open to you in teaching. It keeps your finger on the pulse of the day-to-day management of the school. The job multiskills you and equips you for senior management career progression.

I was tempted by alternative titles for the book. They included, 'Tuck your shirt in!', 'Why are you outside my office, Lisa?' or 'Trainers off and shoes on!'. These expressions number just three of an endless repertoire available to you when you choose to become a head of year.

All interested applicants please read on . . .

1 Matching your personal skills with the job description

I found myself in the cardiac unit of a large Essex hospital. I'd been rushed through A & E which, at that time, looked like a curious mixture of a scene from *The Rake's Progress* and The Battle of Culloden.

My anatomy was being prodded and probed by a registrar whose remote manner was about as cold as a witch's teat. He was in the process of wiring me in parallel with the National Grid and appeared incapable of any form of conversation. It was when he was about to attach yet another electrode to my chest, rendering me a human Christmas tree that I enquired of him, 'Do you enjoy your work?' He didn't even bother to look up. He continued trying to jump start my torso and muttered something quite inaudible. I thought I'd try once more to connect with the mute physician, this time with some patter relevant to my circulatory problem. Nil response, to use a medical term. I decided, therefore, to await my impending rendezvous with the Grim Reaper, clueless about what was happening to me.

Having good people skills is an essential prerequisite for any job where you constantly come into contact with Joe Public. Our silent medic had unfortunately undergone a personality bypass leaving him short on communication expertise, an operation that would seriously limit his success in engaging with patients.

As head of year you will constantly draw on your communication talents in your daily routine of working with teaching colleagues, students, parents and support agencies. You should be known as someone who not only articulates information in a clear and purposeful way, but is also seen as a good listener. People should feel that you are approachable and that you will give them some of your valuable time.

If you intend to follow a pastoral career path, then it is absolutely essential that you like kids. These individuals will consume many of your working hours and it is important that, at the end of a particularly challenging week, you do not feel that The Pied Piper of Hamlin was, after all, a great bloke and a trifle misunderstood. Kids will cause you plenty of hard work. After all, the job is about you ensuring that kids have a positive experience of school life. They get themselves into all sorts of situations. They frequently need your help to sort things out. They will say things that will make you roar with laughter or cringe with disappointment. They may behave in a most inimical way, yet they may tell you things that will bring a lump to your throat. Patience, sensitivity and understanding are fundamental qualities you will find apply to all aspects of this job.

You will need a sense of humour if you are to make any success in your new role. It helps you get through the day. If you cannot smile about some things then the job will become intolerable and this will translate in the way you are seen to operate.

People should see you as someone with a practical and realistic attitude towards the job. At the same time you should instil confidence and respect from those with whom you work. Your success as a leader of your year will also include problem-solving skills. These may be as wide-ranging as your ability to be able to sort out disciplinary matters to

formulating an acceptable blueprint for the phased reintro-
duction of a student with a chronic debility. You should be
able to make resolute decisions about certain issues, yet be
prepared to listen and compromise in others.

A key area of your position as year manager is to set high
standards from all with whom you work. You will prove to
your tutors that you are well organized and have a realistic
understanding of the concept of time. Administrative duties
and meeting deadlines should be seen as no problem to you.
On top of your teaching load there will always be casework to
undertake. An already crowded week will mean you will have
to prioritize items on your agenda. There is a curious pleasure
gained from being able to cross off completed tasks from this
list.

Try to keep your desk as clear as possible. This may be a
difficult task since you will be given a sea of paperwork each
week. A tidy desk and office usually reflects that you are
organized and on top of things. It is embarrassing to meet a
parent in an unkempt room that looks as though you could
find anything from a pair of tickets for the maiden voyage of
the Titanic to an Austin A35 gearbox.

The students in your charge will recognize the fact that you
set them boundaries in terms of what is acceptable and
unacceptable behaviour. They look to you to maintain these
standards. Discipline is not to be viewed as taboo in the climate
of awareness and understanding of individuals. Your students
and colleagues will expect this from you.

You are now a middle manager with its associated status.
You will chair meetings and have to be confident in speaking
to large numbers of people. People will consult you for your
advice and expertise. For them to do this with confidence you
will have shown you have earned your stripes.

All of these personal qualities and aptitudes are essential for
you to make a real success of this position. Some of these

credentials will come easily to you. Some will demand that you work at them. You will make mistakes but remember, you won't make those same errors again. The nature of the job implies you will be continuously learning about people. Expect anything.

It's important that we look at these indispensable skills and abilities prescribed for job success. However, we must now see how these prerequisites transfer to the daily experience of being a year head. Your team of tutors help you manage the year group. Tutors act as the keystone of any pastoral system and the quality of their work will reflect on how strong and successful a leader you are. The head of year acts as the catalyst for these tutors. Staff, remember, are harder people to deal with than the kids and will frequently cause you more problems. You will have in your team some super professionals with whom it is a pleasure to work. Unfortunately you will be allocated some whose inertia and lack of motivation will drive you to drink. How they develop in their role as form tutor is down to you. Ensure they are aware of what you expect from them.

I have worked in schools where year heads perceived as being 'strong' are noticeably missed by staff when they are absent for short periods of time. Control and management of the year group becomes confused and problematic. My personal view is that effective heads of year can create a purposeful climate of orderly behaviour and quality of work without their physical presence being needed to enforce these standards.

Acronyms such as EWO, EP and BSP will be new and frequently used additions to your vocabulary. A part of your new life will involve liaising with outside support agencies, the likes of which your fellow heads of department have only read about in their daily newspapers. Knowing when and how to use these contacts effectively will slowly come as you teethe your way into your new management role. It is essential that you maintain positive links with these bodies even though occasionally they may frustrate you by showing a lack of urgency in dealing with matters.

Heads of year must uphold many whole school issues. Your job description will tell you attendance and timekeeping issues are your responsibility. Your tutor team will help you monitor these matters. I am far from being a Luddite and I applaud modern technology being used to record these two elements. However, in days of yore, an attendance was when a bum was on a seat. An absence was, therefore when a bum was not on that seat. Today, information technology systems tell us there are in fact 12 ways to record an absence. I would recommend everyone sings from the same song sheet and is clear about what lozenge to score through or key to press when registering an absence. The detective role you will often play may concern attendance issues. Truancies need to be identified and also the reasons for these absences. I remember regularly checking attendance registers twice a day at an inner London school. It had to be done to keep on top of some appalling truants. They were so good at disappearing from a classroom, they could have doubled as the crew from the Marie Celeste.

Students will often change schools and it is your responsibility to assemble information for pastoral staff in their new school. Similarly it is your duty to request and receive student details from year heads when a child joins your year group. In tandem with this you must have in place a procedure for welcoming the new student into the year. Here you will liaise with the new tutor and also heads of curriculum area. This is all part of ensuring the smooth process of transition.

As a year manager you will need to guarantee that the pastoral camp of the school underpins its academic pillars. The job description will reinforce this in such a way that you will sometimes be given the powerful designation of Director of Learning. You are someone who has records of the personal and academic details of all the students in your charge. Your role is to make certain these records are accurate and updated as the need arises. Again, the information technology system employed to track student progress should be understood by those who use and interpret it. The year manager is thus the driving force for maximizing student achievement. You will once more work in partnership with tutors and heads of subject areas. On a practical note, though I am a supporter of target setting for students, I do feel we are in danger of system overload. I have observed some school target-setting systems that demand up to three targets be written for students per subject per year. One establishment, embarking on target mania insisted on students having three targets per subject, per term. After a year there was a whole page in *The Times Educational Supplement* devoted to job vacancies in that school.

Parents continue to want a written school report that highlights strengths and weaknesses. Year managers not only oversee the compilation of these booklets but also check that tutors have succinctly summarized its contents. You are also to ensure that tutors have included comments about the personal development of the individual. You must then ask them to provide you with a list of students whose reports need remedial attention. A separate list will also help you congratulate those pupils who have tried hard and made splendid progress.

Many years ago, report writing was performed on a student broadsheet. Subject teachers completed this piece of paper one after the other. It was possible to see comments written by your colleagues. There was sometimes a follow my leader mentality accompanying this system. You may feel that Lois Bloomfield is an undisputed recidivist in your lessons and that you would like to communicate this with all who read her report. However, if you were number five at completing the document, you may notice that no one else has referred to her uncivilized tendencies. Not wishing to appear as a teacher with discipline problems, you very often diluted your intended vitriol. Reports generated using today's mechanism helps avoid such practice and you read a true and comprehensive account.

Year managers are charged with the responsibility of compiling special reports on students. These may be confidential summaries of progress, behaviour and attendance used for job references, court reports or information required by social services. These records need to be both honest and truly representative. In your early days in the job it may be wise to ask your line manager to look over your submission, particularly with sensitive issues such as custody or child protection.

Some schools insist their pastoral middle managers play an active role in organizing parent consultation evenings or in structuring ARDs (Academic Review Days) and target-setting sessions. I would advise you do not leave this duty until the eleventh hour. The perpetual moan from your teaching colleagues is they never see the parents with whom they really need to speak. Contact these parents well in advance and remind them their presence at the meeting would be most helpful. Don't be put off by excuses, if they really cannot make that date on their calendar then arrange an alternative time when you can see them. This should only be suggested as a last resort, you have enough to do without extra appointments in your diary.

One memorable parent who would habitually abscond from these meetings was nicknamed by staff 'The Walking Disease'. Each time the head of year or faculty would ask for her presence at a review meeting concerning her errant son Jake, she would plead some mysterious affliction. Her best ones were that she thought she had 'Mauritius anaemia'. Another was that she was so ill, she could suffer a 'connery' any day now. She did, however, miraculously recover enough from both debilities to attend her twice-weekly rendezvous with Mecca bingo.

Some parents will prove as elusive to contact as Osama Bin Laden. A trusty remedy is to telephone them during *Emmerdale* or *Coronation Street*. These parents never respond to answerphone messages or even letters sent by recorded delivery.

An all too commonly frustrating part of your job description is when you attempt to make a leading contribution to the PSHCE programme. You, along with any PSHCE coordinator, are the driving forces behind its success and implementation in your year. You may feel comfortable talking to kids about most things. You see the relevance of this part of the school curriculum. Sadly, many of your colleagues do not share your views and optimism. Your job is to work closely with this curriculum area coordinator and ensure the teaching and support material are both suitable and readily available to those who implement the course. Be warned! These can be testing times and may impact on your sanity.

Most teachers share the same opinions about meetings. There are too many of them. They last too long. Meetings precipitate other meetings. The list of complaints goes on . . . As head of year, your diary will contain many meeting slots. Two essential components of your meetings programme will be the scheduled time when you meet with your tutors and also a regular session for you to meet with your line manager. Communication between you and your tutors will allow information to flow in both directions. You will be able to speak with this group about issues causing concern, matters relating to school policy and topics relating to your year group. They are important dates on your calendar.

If your line manager seems allergic to the two of you meeting up, then remind them of their obligations. They are likely to be the senior managers of the school and should know better. In your early days as year head these meetings should be helpful. They should be able to give you some constructive advice about how to get the best out of certain situations.

Again, information should be seen to move in both directions. They should be positive experiences. Alas, some members of leadership groups will prove as helpful as enteritis on a long-distance coach trip. Some will do all they can to avoid these scheduled meets. They have more excuses than a truanting pupil.

There will be special duties mentioned in your job description that relate specifically to a particular year. Very often it is these responsibilities that have been drawn up when you apply for this job. Year 7 managers will have responsibility for inception of 11-year-old pupils into Key Stage 3. They not only oversee the preparation for this transfer but also ensure this induction process is smooth and problem free. Make sure you understand everything that is required of you for the particular year group in your charge. I worked with a confident new head of Year 7 who overlooked the compilation of the medical profiles of his new pupils.

You should be asked to chair a year council. Tutors will have overseen the election of these tutor group representatives. Year council meetings discuss topics with both year and whole-school implications. They give the students some feeling of being involved in the way a school is run and how it can develop. I have always found such meetings helpful, because they can help you assess the temperature of the year group as well as giving you more time to get to know your students. You will be both heartened and impressed by much of what they have to say. Year council meetings will often filter issues that will need a presentation at full school council sessions. The head of year will supervise the election of the school council members from his/her year.

The school calendar will boast both whole-school and year-specific activities. You have the right to add to these events should either you, your tutor team or the students feel something positive can be gained from the event. Beware of being too ambitious. You may feel it would be good fun to organize a year talent competition and then follow that soon after with an inter-form quiz. These social events take time to shape and put together. Delegate the responsibility for this. Very often your tutors or members of the year council will be prepared to take on the role of coordinators. Ask them to keep you briefed as to their progress, but never leave them with carte blanche.

One final inclusion for the head of year job description in every school is the responsibility for year assemblies (see the next chapter for more on this). Mercifully these are usually once a week. I would recommend you preside over each gathering. It shows you are in charge and it also allows you to speak with your students. Try to get any notices or information over with first before the theme or meaningful message, is delivered by some person or group. I worked with an eccentric and insensitive head of Year 9 who was obsessed with pupils walking on the left around the school. A charming lady from Amnesty International had been invited to speak with the year and delivered a powerful narrative that brought tears to the eyes of many staff and kids. The lady also concluded her delivery with a rather moving poem. The capricious year head then leapt off his seat, shook her hand and loudly proclaimed,

'Well thanks for that Mrs Lawson. That has certainly given us something to think about. Now, remember, before I dismiss you, always keep to the left!'

He was as suited to the job of head of year as the Reverend Ian Paisley is to working in a library.

To summarize

Your job description is likely to include

1. To lead a team of form tutors.
2. To oversee the work done by this tutor team

3. To ensure this team upholds school policies relating to behaviour, uniform, attendance and punctuality.
4. To prepare them for any PSHCE lessons they have to implement.
5. To support the professional development of these tutors.
6. To have a watching brief over the academic progress of individual students and to have strategies in place for dealing with underachievement.
7. To manage the review and target-setting processes for students in that year.
8. To work in tandem with the tutors in keeping accurate and updated records of student welfare and academic performance.
9. To organize and participate in parents consultation evenings and ARDs.
10. To meet with parents to discuss areas of concern should the need arise.
11. To ensure student progress reports are compiled and completed on time.
12. To organize and lead meetings for parents on year-specific issues.
13. To foster a corporate spirit in the year and arrange activities within the year group.
14. To assemble confidential reports and references for students should the need arise.
15. To work closely with Education Welfare so that attendance and student welfare issues are dealt with expeditiously.
16. To liaise with outside support services such as social services, the Schools' Psychological Service, child guidance and the police.
17. To organize the weekly year assembly programme.
18. To work with your tutor team in maintaining discipline in the year group.

19. To meet regularly with your line manager to discuss issues relating to your year group.
20. To liaise with subject teachers in matters relating to your students.
21. To know the students in your charge.
22. To supervise the establishment of a year council and to chair its meetings.
23. To liaise with other schools to ensure the smooth transfer of students.
24. To maintain your nervous system and to have a happy life.

See how many of these skills match the above specification

Patience, sensitivity, interpersonal skills, listening, communication (written and verbal), organizer, administrator, leadership, industry, problem solving, reliability, sense of humour, decision making, honesty, time management, assertiveness, empathy, clarity and the ability to deal with criticism and negativity.

2 Leading your year group

It is absolutely essential that you as head of your year are a credible figure with your flock. You have status in the school and have the power to make things happen. You are a figure of authority and should command respect from the students in your care.

I was visiting a school for interview some years ago. I was anxious to take the temperature of the school in terms of student behaviour. The best thing to do in this case is to visit the boys' loos and check for graffiti. I would not recommend this strategy though if you are female and you want the job. If you read statements like 'Mrs Dolan is a toser' inscribed in magic marker on the back of a toilet door or comments such as 'Mr Parsons is a count' it tells you two things. First, the scrawl was penned by a Year 7 student – Years 8 to 11 would have omitted the title. Second, it would seem to vindicate the need for a literacy hour.

I had just turned into the main school corridor and I immediately became aware that there was trouble at t' mill. A rather young, and I would suggest inexperienced head of year was delivering an almighty verbal lashing to a lofty Year 11 student in front of several fellow Year 11s. The member of staff's delivery was not dissimilar to that of Adolf Hitler on a night out at the Reichstag. His gesticulations would have been the envy of a racecourse tic-tac man. I could see this tirade was having very little affect on the youth and his aco-lytes too seemed similarly unimpressed. To cap it all and make the head of year look a veritable pilchard in front of his adolescent audience, a Year 9 pupil walked past the altercation, bouncing a football. Just as the teacher was concluding his admonishment by shouting, 'Now do you understand what I've been saying, Gary Reilly?' the student calmly said to the passing boy, 'On me head Warren!'

Kids will often attempt to wind you up. It's part of their job description. You must avoid 'losing it' with students. You tend to lose your self-respect and dignity if you do. Kids find this behaviour a weakness and they will not take you seriously. There's a time and a place for raising your voice, which can be quite effective if reserved for special occasions.

You should keep to the teachers' code of being firm but fair. By the term firm, I do not mean that you should run a Draconian regime. Wackford Squeers did not keep a happy work environment. Fairness too does not mean you being the year doormat. The pupils should be made aware of what you expect from them and how they should relate to others. They should understand the behaviour you will and will not accept. Laying these foundations can be difficult. You don't want to come across as too authoritative because you need to be approachable. Students need to be able to feel they can discuss often personal and sensitive issues with you, particularly if they cannot connect with their tutor. They need to trust you. If you say you are going to do something, they will expect you to do it. False and empty promises disappoint children and lose their support and trust. Establishing yourself with a year group will take time. However, you do need to set these important boundaries and grow with the year group before you blend in other personal qualities.

Students need to believe you are aware of everything that is going on in the year. If they are convinced of this then they are less likely to get up to mischief. If you do not know all that is taking place behind the scenes then pretend you do. It's also useful to have a group of narks from whom you can call in a favour every now and then. There is an unwritten law among pupils that they never 'grass each other up'. However, if you have a good working relationship with your year group and are seen as equitable and decent, then it's amazing just how many whispers you will hear. When you have to investigate some incident, never see a group of students together. First choose which students you need to question and then separate them. I recall isolating five pupils in different areas around the school when a drugs episode needed thorough attention. This meant they were unable to speak with each other and establish a story. In this way each student does not know what the others have told you and it's far easier to establish a complete picture of what has happened. In this particular incident it took me about an hour to discover the felon and where he'd stashed some cannabis resin the size of a house brick.

I feel it is also prudent that you visit your tutor groups as much as possible during tutor time. This will be useful in two ways. First, it allows you to discover what is going on during this important part of the school day. Are your tutors doing the business or doing their lottery numbers? Second, it enables you to have greater contact with the year. The more frequently they see you the more they believe you are in touch with what's going on. After all, we as teachers believe senior management doesn't know what's going on in a school if they aren't seen around the corridors. It enables you to undertake spot checks on uniform or jewellery. It gives you a few minutes to speak to tutors and their group. You can also use this slot for giving recognition to students who have achieved something in or out of school. You can spend some of this time looking at students' work. Praise and congratulations for a piece of work from the head of year means a lot to kids. I must inject a word of caution here. The topography of some schools means that tutor rooms are often scattered in all corners of the school. Don't give yourself a thrombie as you strive to attend all eight classes in 20 minutes. Be realistic, visit some today and the rest tomorrow. It's your regular presence that counts.

It is a reality that you will never be given enough non-contact time enabling you to do the job. You will be forced into using your morning break and lunchtimes to complete your tasks for the day. I remember one head of house who would never undertake any pastoral work during the lunch hour. His sandwiches and coffee would appear at the beginning of lunch followed by a 45-minute stab at the *Telegraph* crossword. He would remain inaccessible each lunchtime. The bell for afternoon registration would then sound and off he'd waddle back to his office. The gentleman was not on top of his job and the year group suffered accordingly. At the risk of my teaching union demanding my blood for such heresy, I must point out I am not advocating you should never have a lunch break. I simply believe the head of year job will frequently encroach into your break times. It is the nature of the job. We need to see students during the course of the school day.

It is always wise to know what is happening in the playground or on the school field during break and lunchtimes. You know your potential Feltham young offender element in your year. At the risk of imitating Donald Rumsfeld, make sure that you know, that they know, that you know etc. . . . how they pass the time. You should know who are your smokers, your gamblers, your potential bullies, graffiti artists and vandals. You should also know where they are likely to be at these times. A quick stroll around the trouble spots of the school every now and then helps. It's often amazing what you discover. I once turned a quiet corner at the back of the technology block to discover Murdoch Singh (his dad was Punjabi and his mother from Dunoon) practising ballet steps with his new girlfriend Eunice Batty, with whom he was totally besotted. Murdoch, I must add, was 'the man' in Year 11 and ruled mercilessly. Witnessing this scene allowed me to call in a few markers from him in the future. What a result!

Your fellow professionals will often judge you by the year you run. Don't be upset by some throwaway remarks made by some insensitive staff about either you or the year. Remember, you are doing the hardest job in the school and they aren't! You may have inherited a group from a year manager who suffered constant narcolepsy. This lot will need immediate attention. Nobody will be expecting you to change them overnight into holy order candidates. If you work hard with that group to make them raise their game you will gain respect from your colleagues and also the pupils themselves. Situations like this will mean a slow process of recovery.

Establishing yourself with a group of 200 students also demands you create a feeling of corporate spirit and identity among this large group. Kids need to feel they belong to their year group. There should be a sense of pride in the year. You cannot achieve this on your own. The tutor team must support you and reinforce the work you do. Sports day, tutor group assemblies and inter-form competitions constitute the usual demands of the school calendar which you and your tutor team organize and oversee. Kids really appreciate those extra special events peculiar to their year. If you manage Year 11, then organize a souvenir year book, compiled and edited by the students. Commemorate the milestone of them finishing their period of compulsory schooling by arranging a leavers' dinner and dance. Get the students involved in its preparation and planning (but no assessment!).

Most year groups will have their own year assembly once a week. The year manager is usually in charge of this gathering. Themes for the assembly are frequently designed to dovetail with material covered in PSHCE. However, you as year head should be influential in its compilation and have a strong say in the programme. It may be that some incident has occurred and you feel it needs air time in an assembly. You may want to devolve some responsibility for an assembly to tutors. I would strongly recommend this. Delegation is not a dirty word. Some tutors will need help in this task. On no account allow their tutees to have a free rein, otherwise the final product could be embarrassing and do your credibility no good at all. I witnessed one tutor group assembly many years ago that was not only tasteless but was downright offensive. The head of year had given carte blanche to a tutor who was in great need of support in his form-tutor role and also with his wayward group. The chap was incredibly naïve about most aspects of life. His group told me their tutor thought lap dancing took place in a country in Scandinavia! The assembly predictably slipped into a sea of bad language and poor taste. Not good at all for anyone!

Your assembly deliveries should be well prepared and executed. You are the principal player in that year and you should set an example to all. Tutors will be watching you to see how it's done. The students will watch and listen to your words (that's the theory anyway). I recall a fellow year head, not long in post, who twice got people's names wrong in his morning assembly story. He looked rather forlorn as he was dismissing the students at the end of the gathering. 'Don't worry about gettin' them names wrong, Sir!' were words of comfort from Zuleema Meredith – a Year 10 girl with a big heart and mouth to match. 'They probably weren't listenin' anyway.'

The same chap a couple of months later was about to conclude his message for the morning assembly when he saw a pupil blowing a huge chewing-gum bubble. He stopped his humanitarian theme mid-flow and verbally savaged the miscreant for a good 30 seconds. He then looked down at his notes and concluded the gathering with 'Lord, give us patience to be kind to one another.'

Use these assembly spots for giving praise as well as instruction. Again, you should know what is going on within your year. There will be students for whom academic achievement does not come easy. However, these youngsters may be successful in things they undertake outside school. Recognition of this fact can be given during this assembly time. It is essential that your tutors keep you up to speed with such information. They should actively encourage youngsters to keep a record of their own personal achievements in their personal development folders.

Do not go it alone with an assembly programme. Such a practice is unhelpful for three reasons. First, it is absolutely impossible to discover fresh and engaging material each week for five years! Second, your constant weekly attempt to embody Demosthenes will prove tedious with your congregation. Third, it prevents staff and students, who would like to contribute to the now moribund corporate climate, from doing so. Memories of a man who adhered to such convention haunt me like Yossarian's dream. His pace, monotone and delivery made Wayne Rooney sound like Stephen Fry. Years of uninspiring and wearisome repetition gave rise to a year group with a distinct lack of *joie de vivre*.

A sound tip is to make a note of assembly material you use and when. This will prevent you delivering the same theme and message to a group who have heard it before. You'll soon gather you've made a faux pas if there is an initial period of muttering followed by shuffling around on their seats. Always be on the look out for new material for assemblies. Newspaper articles, music, exemplar books on assembly topics and the internet are all possible sources. Poach good assembly ideas from colleagues. They won't object as long as you don't use it the day before they do.

One special skill that has developed alongside the changing

role of heads of year is to be able to cope with the increase in the amount of information about the pupils in our care. It is our job to collate and scrutinize information about the whole child. How easy this task is depends upon the information management system of the school. The use of ARDs and target-setting sessions means it is essential that performance information is regularly fed into the system. The head of year and their tutor team will then consolidate the data for each child and trawl through this sea of information. It is a time-consuming yet purposeful undertaking. Heads of department will frustrate you when their data fails to go onto the system. Some of them will wonder what all the fuss is about and be completely oblivious to deadlines as they see you swallow your third Temazepam. It is worth reinforcing these dates for completion alongside the school's published times with a personal reminder note well in advance. You will slowly become aware which heads of department need reminding about calendars and time.

Performance spreadsheets of students furnish the necessary information for highlighting underachievement and provide raw data for target-setting programmes. They link into IEPs. They are used to look for patterns or trends. They track student progress from baseline assessment in primary schools through the SATS years to GCSE. This data can be used for all kinds of exercises from looking at gender differences in achievement through to fortune telling about performance at the key stages. Keeping on top of such information mechanisms is an extremely important aspect of the job.

Record keeping also embraces coping with attendance statistics. Schools now have information technology programmes in place designed to help tutors and heads of year stay in control of attendance and punctuality matters. Make sure you know how the system works and make the system work for you. Ensure it gives you the relevant data when you want it. Attendance monitoring depends upon accurate

information being fed into the system by tutors and classroom teachers. If rubbish is put into the programme then you
will get inaccurate information out of the system. Stress
the urgency and importance of reliable data input to these
people.

Your students will test you and the system to see if they can
truant or keep poor time. If such acts remain undetected or
lack remedial attention then you are perceived quite rightly as
not being in control of your year. Ensure that notes are
recorded, dated and filed. Do not allow notes explaining
absences to be thrown away. Check the administrative staff are
dealing with these records correctly. You as the year manager
are responsible for producing this information at important
times. These will include student case conferences, suspension
appeals hearings, court attendance and for student references.
All of these instances will require accurate and often detailed
statistics.

It is essential that you keep on top of these attendance
issues and act swiftly when the need arises. Schools have a
policy for dealing with student attendance. You should know
who are your poor attenders. You will soon be aware of your
students who suffer from bed sores and cannot get into school
on time. Office staff frequently deal with telephone calls concerning student absence. This will include 'first day calling'
procedure. It is sometimes wise to alert the office administrative staff of your concerns about attendance or punctuality of
certain students. A colleague reminded me of a telephone call
taken by a member of the school office team. The conversation took the following course:

Office: 'Good morning, thank you for phoning Sidney
Thomas School, Janice Roberts speaking. How can I help
you?'

Person: 'Oh! Er. Er. I'm phoning to say that Dean Ricketts
isn't comin' to school today 'cos he's not well.'

Office: 'Dean?' queried the receptionist. 'That's you Dean, isn't it?' persisted the alert lady.

Person: (Yes, you guessed it too!) 'Er, er, er. No, it's me Dad!' concluded Dean. Bad luck Deano, sussed!

A considerable proportion of your time will be taken by having to deal with discipline and behavioural issues. Remember, discipline is shaping an acceptable code of conduct in which certain attitudes are allowed to develop. It is not ranting and raving at students with a volume equivalent to a market trader. Similarly it is not bullying a year group. Common incidents with which you will frequently deal are skirmishes between the students themselves. It could be an altercation between a student and a teacher or form tutor. The head of year is always summoned to arbitrate when a crisis occurs between senior management and one of your year group. It could be a conflict between a parent and their progeny. From time to time you will be asked to remedy poor behaviour from your students with the general public. Situations like these will draw upon all your human resources skills. You will slowly become proficient at dealing with these problems. You will need to respond professionally and remember to separate the act from the person. Try to think ahead with matters concerning poorly behaved students. Have preventative strategies in place. Ask yourself, 'What might happen if . . . ?'

One superlative quality that must be shown by every year head is the ability to listen to youngsters. They will tell you all sorts of things if they respect and trust you. You may be having a bad or busy day. For some reason they have chosen you in order to offload something that's been on their minds. It may be something that is quick and easy to remedy. Sometimes it is a matter that will demand half an hour of your already crowded day. The important thing is that you should give them that time. If it cannot be attended to at that moment, then you must create a slot for them. If it's urgent, then see them sometime on that day. If, from what they've briefly outlined, you both think it will keep until the next day, then that's fine. The important skill here is that you show you are prepared to listen to their problem and that they feel comfortable discussing their difficulties with you.

To summarize

The way students should see you as head of year

1. You embody everything about the year group in your charge.
2. You set the high standards of work and behaviour that you expect from them.
3. Your year group respect you for the way you are seen to work.
4. You are a firm but fair individual.
5. You listen to the students in your charge.
6. You oversee the day-to-day running of mutually supportive tutor teams.
7. You are perceived as multiskilled in that you seem to deal effectively with many different tasks.
8. You are an enabler, and the kids in your charge see that you can make things happen.
9. You are to be trusted. If you say you are going to do something, then it gets done.
10. You are seen as someone who can help students sort out their problems.
11. You are on top of important issues such as attendance and punctuality.
12. You are accessible and approachable.
13. You speak well in public.
14. You recognize student achievement in all its forms.

15. You know how much progress students are making in their subjects.
16. You know what is going on in your year.
17. You don't appear to flap in times of crisis.
18. You have status within the school.

3 Leading your tutor team

Starting a new teaching job part way through a school year in January is difficult enough at the best of times. Taking on the role of head of year in a place where you do not know the staff or the students is certainly an experience that is guaranteed to rapidly remove memories of Christmas pudding and goodwill to all.

I was to start as head of Year 10 at my new school in inner London. I would be in charge of some 200 students and lead a tutor team of eight. In common with ends of term in most large comprehensive schools, there had been no slackening in work rate towards the end of this pre-Christmas period. Parents unknowingly irritate teachers by making innocent, yet ill-informed remarks such as,

'Oh, I suppose with there being a couple of weeks left until the end of term, you'll be winding down now?' Winding down? It was manic right until the first warm glass of Cava had been gratefully quaffed at the staff bash on the last day.

Prior to taking up this position I had only been given the opportunity to meet with six of my new tutors. Two of them were leaving to take up jobs in new schools. This initial meeting with the rest of the team was rather brief and merely an opportunity to introduce myself. Unfortunately, this can sometimes happen with posts of pastoral responsibility. The essential preparation work you need to undertake with the staff and students is often overlooked by senior management. Make sure you insist this does not happen.

I had met the previous year head who was preoccupied with thoughts of treading the fairways during his impending retirement. He gave me a rapid and somewhat anaemic over-view of the year. He'd led them since their secondary school inception in Year 7. Similarly, he raced through the strengths and weaknesses of his tutor team. The two tutors I would lose, according to this Tiger Woods groupie, were no loss to any-one. His rapid and cursory analysis meant there would be problems with their tutor groups.

I arrived at the school at 7.30 am on this first day of the spring term. Unfortunately there was no training day to allow me to meet my team before the term started. That would have to wait until the end of school. One of my new tutors was a former supply who had worked at the school and knew her tutor group. She'd covered them many times before. My other recruit was a Mrs Lythgoe, a timorous lady whose CV boasted over ten years of secondary experience. In retrospect, I feel it must have been in empty schools. I met her for the first time five minutes before the start of morning registration. I decided to accompany her to the tutor room and chat along the way.

There was a classroom D2 at the end of a corridor. This was to be her new home with 10L. It soon became clear that we were in bandit country by the degree of noise and unrest emanating from the aforementioned room. We were ten yards from the door when a male body wearing nothing but trou-sers and trainers was propelled from the room on his bottom. The young man whose frail torso resembled a white toast rack was completely oblivious to our presence. He picked himself up, shouted to the animated crew within and ran back to join the action.

It was at this point Mrs Lythgoe froze. She seemed incapable of any movement in her lower limbs. However, I sensed from her pallor that there was movement elsewhere in her anatomy. She grabbed my arm and held onto it tightly. Her grip on me was so tight that she was in the process of occluding the blood supply to my wrist and fingers. After what seemed to be an hour of her anaesthetising my left arm, she looked up at me in terror and said, 'You're not going to leave me with this lot, are you?'

We will all meet a Mrs Lythgoe during our lives as head of year. There are some of your colleagues who need very little support as form tutors. They, like you, seem to be on auto-pilot when it comes to dealing with their tutees. Some, however, the Mrs Lythgoes, will take up much of your time in terms of guidance and encouragement.

One very common issue you will have to deal with is that some teachers feel being a form tutor is an imposition. They believe they are paid to teach their subject specialism and they really haven't the time to bother with all of this pastoral nonsense. They weren't trained as form tutors and so why should they bother? This minority group are, perhaps, the most challenging of all tutors you are likely to meet. Registers are dutifully completed but there is no rapport with their group. The kids themselves see these tutors as openly lazy. These individuals will try to do the bare minimum and will succeed if you do not address the problem. I cannot understand why these individuals bother to enter the teaching profession. When you become a teacher you take on the whole job package and being a form tutor is an essential element of your teaching experience. It is important that such apathy and negativity is addressed. It is easier for you to achieve a change in such recalcitrants when they are the lone voice in a mutually supportive and progressive team.

Getting the best out of your tutor team involves recognizing their individual needs and personal circumstances. Some will feel confident in handling certain issues but will need help from you in others. They may sense they are limited in some skills and that it is this part of the job that gives them the greatest challenge. It is your duty as head of year to work with these teachers. Your role is to boost their confidence and raise their morale. They see you tackle your job with confidence. They feel you have all of the strategies in place for dealing with all kinds of problems. Again, you are to act as a catalyst for these tutors and raise their self-esteem. You can make them believe in themselves and give them confidence in whatever they do. In time, their professional skills will grow and develop. It is your support, input and guidance that will have managed this change.

A tutor who is fragile in their role will respond well to praise and congratulation when they have achieved something. It is a tactic we use with our students. If they have followed up a questionable student absence or helped you collate the necessary paperwork of an incident concerning one of their tutor group, then a thank you is much appreciated. Spend some time with them explaining the need for such investigation and procedure. They will then understand the importance of such actions.

Giving tutors support, frequently means listening to them. If you are approachable and have their respect for the way you operate it will be easier for them to seek advice from you. They may feel unhappy implementing some PSHCE material. You may well decide that a team teaching approach provides a suitable prescription for helping them through that particular difficulty. Someone may need assistance in coping day to day with a particular student. Provide such support for them but do not constantly give this same help. Allow them to learn from you and how you tackle these problems. It is an essential part of their professional learning experience.

I was returning to my office and found Edson Rowntree leaning against the wall outside my room. 'Hello Edson, do you want to see me?' I inquired. He looked down at the ground and muttered,

'Yes, Sir. Mr Oluwayu sent me. He told me to wait outside your room.' Ruben Oluwayu was a charming man in his second year of teaching. He was slowly getting to grips with being a form tutor but lacked confidence in dealing firmly with lairy students. If a discipline issue took place in his tutor group, he would panic and send the student to me instead of dealing with the matter himself.

'Why did he send you out?' was my second question.

''Cos I said you're an arsehole, Sir,' was his mumbled reply.

'Me?' was my startled response.

'No, not you Sir. Leroy Javine. He was cussin' my mum,' Edson nervously explained.

It took some time to coach Ruben in behaviour management. His confidence slowly improved. He was grateful for such assistance and he became one of my most reliable and loyal tutors.

Remember, it is not your job to do everything concerning your year group. You have a tutor team to help you run the year. This involves you delegating meaningful responsibility for many duties. Delegation is not a dishonourable word. It is not a weakness, it is a strength. Tutors should have a clear understanding of their job description and it is your duty to ensure these tasks are carried out. You cannot carry passengers because the students suffer. Your tutors should share your own pastoral vision.

Schools should have a job description available for form tutors. Such specification needs to be very clear about what these duties entail. When you take up the post of head of year I would suggest you keep a copy so that you are aware of what the school expects from them and that you will be perceived to be working in accordance with the rest of the pastoral system. I have known some maverick year heads make unreasonable demands on tutors who already have a full workload. Each year will have its own demands unique to that year cohort. These duties should be sewn into that standard job description.

I have read examples of form-tutor responsibilities in different schools. The initial requirement common to all of these models is that the form tutor is to act as the first point of contact between the home and school. This communication is to be by letter, telephone or in person. I would inject a few words of caution here. In no way should you allow communication to take place without you being aware of this, particularly if you are unsure as to the competency of the tutor. Insist that records of these communications are made available to you and are then filed. This procedure is designed to help the tutor as well as keep you in the picture as to what is happening with a particular student. It can come as a shock, when at a tutor team meeting, a tutor discloses some important information relating to a student that is already three weeks old!

As part of this communication process, you should ask your tutors to remain vigilant and look for any patterns of student behaviour. They should notice anything that appears out of the ordinary. I also refer to scrutinizing absence notes and notifications of impending medical visits. You will already be aware of the students in your charge who can forge a £20 note. However, it can be quite alarming when you uncover a range of truancies from a student whose behaviour you considered to be as virtuous as the Pope.

Parents will often disclose personal information that is impacting on their son's or daughter's life at school. It is essential that your tutor, who is on the receiving end of this news, relays it to you. It may be that you consider this tutor is able to deal with this situation and keep you informed. However, it may well be an issue that needs your input. This may take the form of you sitting in on meetings with the parents or you precipitating contact with support agencies. The important thing is the tutor does not feel alone in dealing with this matter. You have been there to give support and advice.

It also follows that any information you acquire about a student must be passed on to the tutor. In some instances if the matter has serious implications it will be necessary to inform your own line manager. Information sharing is thus a two-way process.

It is important to explain to your tutors the necessity of keeping an accurate attendance and punctuality register. They record this essential information twice a day. Stress the use of such data and give examples. It can be acutely embarrassing if the figures you are using during an attendance investigation are incorrect. It will also not impress Education Welfare if you discover that a student with an unblemished set of attendance figures has had more days off than Andy Capp. All of your tutors must follow the same school blueprint for recording and monitoring this information. Ensure the attendance register is completed by the tutor and not by some pupil conscript. Stress that it is a legal document and will need to be produced in a court of law if attendance problems with students necessitate such action. Recording attendance should be undertaken in silence to avoid mistakes being made.

I was passing a tutor room one morning and a supply teacher was attempting to call the tutor register. He was experiencing much difficulty in making sense of responses because of the high levels of background noise.

'Every time I open my mouth, some idiot speaks!' he bellowed. The background din was instantly reinforced with riotous laughter and the art of precise attendance recording that day went rapidly out of the window.

If you work in a school that has a uniform or dress code it falls to the pastoral system to be the principal champions of such guidelines. Tutors are the first wave of uniform monitors. They see the students as they arrive in the mornings. They should ensure their flock leave this morning tutor gathering suitably booted and suited. Similarly when they arrive for afternoon roll call, it is the tutor's duty to supervise the meta-morphosis from partially clad, trainer-wearing hobos into pris-tine, sartorially elegant members of the species Homo sapiens.

Another chore you expect from your tutor team members is they are to check homework is being set and recorded. The majority of schools insist that such information is recorded in homework diaries or planners. It is a duty that adds to an already crowded list but it is an essential enterprise for two reasons. It allows you to see that homework is being set by subject teachers. It also allows parents to monitor this work and gives them an opportunity to communicate with the school. Ask your tutors to give a careful eye as to what is and what is not recorded in this booklet. Ask them to look for patterns such as persistent failure to set any homework. Could it be students failing to record the work or is the subject teacher persistently not setting any work? Look for comments from parents that may give you this valuable information. It may be the homework set by a subject teacher took many hours to complete in one evening and left no time for other work.

The planner is an important two-way communication between home and school. If these planners are not examined by tutors, then it really looks bad on you and the school if a parent discovers that certain homework is not being set. As a final suggestion, ensure a parent's signature is inspected by your tutors. I once knew a talented Year 9 calligraphist who charged 50p per forgery from his year mates.

One dramatic change recently introduced is ARDs. A whole raft of information is now available about the student, ready for discussion with parents. Tutors must survey this broadsheet in advance of this meeting. In tandem with this, any student who needs remedial attention or praise should be brought to your notice. You cannot be expected to trawl through over 200 spreadsheets in great detail. Their task is to filter this sea of information. The tutor is the linchpin of this performance review and target-setting procedure. Some tutors are very reliable and do this undertaking with ease and skill. Be mindful of the few who may rush this exercise. Make sure they give it the time it deserves. Your duty as head of year is to ensure data reaches them in good time. Here, you rely on subject leaders to meet the prescribed deadlines. Your function is to protect and look after your team by liaising with these fellow middle managers, thereby guaranteeing the punctuality of this information.

In the majority of secondary schools, tutors are still expected to complete tutor reports. These are usually summative comments on student progress in lessons but also give a broader picture of their performance and personal development. Subject colleagues often use statement banks to provide information. Tutors will need to spend time reading these often impersonal and cursory sentences. They are then expected to crystallize any advice and recommendations and convey this information as a tutor report. The pastoral report, as it was once known, will need to be supplemented with student achievement outside the classroom together with how the student is developing as an individual. It demands knowledge of the student and this is why your tutors should be encouraged to observe, talk with and listen to their tutees. In this way, tutor reports become truly representative and have both meaning and purpose.

Heads of year must check these tutor comments for content, spelling and grammar. Spelling 'focused' or 'focussed' has baffled report writers for years and is par for the course. The word 'conscientious' continues to outwit members of the PE department. When reports were in longhand, it was the written word 'work' that frequently resembled the slang term for masturbation. Partly legible comments reading 'He has been wanking well throughout the year' did not provide parents with any optimism. I also remember reading some ironic mis-spelling and scrawl from a SEN teacher whose advice read 'Liam writes erotically'. Clearly, Liam would be a future Mills and Boon contributor.

Perhaps one of the most troublesome aspects of tutoring is the implementation and delivery of PSHCE. Some schools employ a PSHCE coordinator whose job is to oversee its teaching across the whole school. They may use specialist teams of teachers together with outside speakers to articulate this area of the curriculum. In others, it is down to the tutors to teach the majority of the syllabus for that year.

The universal moan from tutors is that they feel unquali-fied to teach topics such as 'gender issues in the world of work', or 'problems with relationships'. Another issue is that any training or support material is either in short supply or never quite in place. I am sure you have been faced with many a PSHCE lesson where the worksheets or video accompany-ing the subject matter, both of which you've never seen, arrive either ten minutes before the lesson starts, or in many cases it appears ten minutes before the lesson is about to finish. For PSHCE to have a credible status in the school curriculum its delivery, content, resourcing and coordination have to be given a high priority. Tutors and the students themselves have been given a raw deal with PSHCE for years. The year head must have a major input into this dimension in both support and the training of tutors.

The same kind of help and advice needs to be there when it comes to organizing tutor group activities and teams. Some of the tutors you will meet are natural organizers. They inject tremendous energy into these events. Other tutors will be lukewarm and clueless. It is these, often feckless characters, who will need close scrutiny. Ensure they are made clear of your requirements well in advance. This should often involve guidance notes and a structure for completing the task. Follow this with requests for progress updates.

The composition of tutor groups can sometimes make it harder or easier for the tutor and you should be sensitive to this. If the group is composed of 25 giant amoebae then sports day team success will be limited. Nevertheless, as some Corinthian clueless about kids once decreed, 'It's the taking part that counts!' Some consolation for a tutor and his tutees as the group are seen finishing the 1800 metres just in time for News at Ten!

I would include tutor group assemblies as examples of events that need careful preparation. It is not enough to give your tutor a date for the assembly and then leave them to their own devices. You should be aware of the subject or theme of the assembly and how it is going to be delivered, well in advance of that time. If you have concerns about any of this, then you should tell the tutor so. Remember, you embody your year. You are Year 10 and nothing should antagonize your hard work or the image of the year.

Your tutors should try to involve as many students as possible in the assembly production. There is, however, no need to have a cast the size of *Lord of the Rings*. Some students work better behind the scenes arranging props or music. The essential point is that the end product is a commendable corporate exercise with a meaningful message delivered to the front and rear stalls. Your après-assembly duty is then to congratulate the tutor and their class for all of their efforts. This final act really does count and makes the stress, anxiety and stage nerves all seem to have been worthwhile.

Form tutors should be given encouragement to attend INSET on pastoral issues. These sessions are an opportunity to remedy weaknesses. When you speak with your fellow heads of year you will discover they too will have tutors with similar needs. As a group you should inform your line managers of these needs and ask for slots in training days to be made available enabling these areas to be addressed. INSET sessions and training days are about responding to these needs. Make sure you give them plenty of advanced notice. Training days are all too frequently absorbed by discussing new initiatives, and little time is left for bread and butter issues. These sessions are cheap to organize and can focus on day-to-day problems experienced by tutors.

Some training on more specialist topics tend to be best delivered extramurally. There may be tutors who show potential in pursuing pastoral middle management. You should support their aspirations by alerting the staff facilitator for continuous professional development.

Year team meetings will have to fit into already busy weeks. It is vital that these meetings are part of the school meetings calendar and not hastily arranged by you on an ad hoc basis. All your tutors are expected to attend and if these dates are on the menu there will be no place for excuses such as 'I have an origami team practice at that time!' These get-togethers are important occasions when information can flow both ways. The sessions allow you to focus on matters you believe are essential to keep the year group ticking over. They should also provide your tutors with an opportunity to discuss concerns. The danger with these gatherings is that time can often be wasted on discussing a single student. Detailed concerns over individual students are best dealt separately with the tutor.

Give your tutors an agenda well in advance of these meetings so that they have an opportunity to think about issues. As you visit your tutor groups you can also ask tutors if they have anything they feel merits discussion at the future meeting. If you feel they highlight an issue that is worth air time, then include it in the main agenda and don't squeeze it into AOB. Allocate a certain amount of time for each topic. Do not get sidetracked. Do not overcrowd your agenda. Yes, you will have to use some of this time for disseminating information, but ensure it is not a monologue.

One final note concerns the naming of tutor groups. Schools usually choose the first letter of the tutor's surname. I have known some schools choose the first letter of both first and surname of the tutor. Beware! A friend of mine assumed the reins of a Year 10 group and advised them they were to be known as 10GG. The proclamation produced howls of laughter from Gujarati-speaking boys in the group. Apparently the word sounding like GG in Gujarati means large breasts!

Your tutor team will enable you to work more effectively. They will demand from you honesty and openness. You should expect the same from them. As with the students in your charge, you should be a credible leader who creates a mutually supportive climate seen to be underpinned by your hard work and care for all those associated with your year.

To summarize

What you should expect from your tutors:

1. To act as the first point of contact between home and school.
2. To keep an accurate attendance register and to monitor the attendance and punctuality of the students in their charge.
3. To receive notes from home regarding student absence, hospital/medical visits, problems at home, problems with work, etc.
4. To record these communications and to pass on to the head of year important information or correspondence.
5. To monitor students' academic progress and to participate in target-setting procedures.

6. To contribute to the maintenance of accurate records of their students and to update these records when required.
7. To check homework diaries/planners on a regular basis.
8. To check the standards of dress and uniform of members of their tutor group.
9. To write tutor reports on the pupils in their tutor group.
10. To attend the scheduled pastoral team meetings.
11. To be willing to participate in INSET on relevant pastoral issues.
12. To organize tutor-group activities, team events and assemblies.
13. To talk and listen to members of their group. To be approachable.
14. To be present at interviews with parents.
15. To implement tutorial work and PSHCE
16. To maintain discipline within the tutor group.
17. To have a sense of humour and to still be able to teach after undertaking all of the above.

What your tutors expect from you:

1. To be a credible manager and leader of the year group.
2. To work hard and to know most of the answers.
3. To be respected by the year group for the way you tackle your job.
4. To set high standards of work and behaviour from the pupils.
5. To treat tutors as individuals and to recognize their needs, strengths and weaknesses.
6. To be honest and open about issues.
7. To be approachable and to be a good listener.
8. To give them time and support with certain problems.

9. To give them praise or recognition for anything they do well.

10. To boost their morale and to raise their self-esteem.

11. To respect their opinions, even though they may be different to your own. Not to bear grudges.

12. To show fundamental qualities such as tact and diplomacy.

13. To be unflappable even after you've had a mother of a day!

4 Working with parents

I am indebted to my uncle Horace once more for yet another expression he would sometimes use. Unfortunately, the quote from this dotard, involved a further reference to urinary behaviour.

'I'll tell thee lad,' was his learned introduction, 'I'd sooner have them inside the tent weein' out, than outside the tent weein' in!' He would impart much erudite information to me in my formative years, a great deal of it rather disappointingly, was concerned with excretory habits.

My reason for reflecting on such discerning philosophy is to point out a home–school partnership should exist in all schools. Schools should be seen to work with parents and to share the same goals. In this way we can overcome any feelings of suspicion and negativity from both parties.

Improving home–school relationships brings important mutual benefits to children and their families, and to schools and their communities. The head of year is an integral part of this union. His or her optimism and participation in this practice should cascade down to the tutor teams.

Teachers are sometimes guilty of complaining about parents in that they lack expertise in school matters or they are over-concerned with trivialities. Parents always seem to complain and never praise. They sometimes feel that parents are too conservative about educational ideas and are only too quick to offload responsibility for their child's education onto the school. Building a positive and cooperative home–school ethos tears down these barriers

We have to be mindful of the fact that for parents, many years have passed since they had any dealings with schools. It may be that they were left with unhappy memories of their period of compulsory education. A school's mission today is to make parents feel welcome when they come to the school. They should also be encouraged to contact the school should the need arise. For some parents, coming up to the school is an unnerving experience. I have known parents have a tipple before attending a parental interview to give them some confidence. One parent I knew had so much tipple he forgot about what it was he wanted to complain.

I recall a couple of parents whose visit to the school turned out to be far from a positive experience. I was showing a couple around the school who wanted their daughter, Crystal Duxbury, to join Year 9. According to them, she'd been bullied in her present school and they believed she needed a change. My impression of Crystal, gained from a 20-minute interview and a quick trip around the school, was that she had the self-confidence of Genghis Khan with a morphology to match. Most pupils would sooner chew glass than bully her.

We were nearly half-way through our tour of the school when the positive and welcoming experience was quickly arrested. A Year 11 student Ali Yalcin, an habitual truant, was hiding in the boys' toilets during this stage of the day. On hearing my voice, he hurriedly scaled the WC, raised a panel in the suspended ceiling and secreted himself in the loft space. Unfortunately for Ali and, as it turned out Mrs Duxbury too, he scorched his rear on a steam pipe. The pain reflex caused him to tumble through the ceiling. His rapid fall to earth showered Crystal and her dad with plaster and fibreboard. His descent was also by way of Mrs Duxbury, her bouffant hairstyle and bosom, rendering her supine on the tiled floor. Crystal did not join our school roll, much to the relief of Year 9. Ali continued to truant.

When you interview parents, whether it's at your request or at their own, it is so important you listen to what they have to say. Try and see the world from their perspective. This may be difficult, particularly if they are wearing blinkers at the time. Some parents will find it difficult to articulate their thoughts and ideas. Some, however, will speak with the fluency of Cicero. Whatever their delivery, listen to and understand what they have to say.

Some parents get themselves fired up before the meeting and really let fly from the instant they sit down with you. Be patient. Never lose your temper and start shouting at them. You lose dignity and self-respect if this happens. If they decide to roar, then that's down to them. Be calm and gently remind them that you understand they are upset but shouting is not the way to address these issues.

You should be pleasant, courteous and polite even though you are tempted to tell them where they should insert their opinions. Be careful of your own body language. No pointing or arm waving please, this is unacceptable. I was once spoken to, or perhaps semaphored to, by a parent with more arm movements than John Travolta in *Saturday Night Fever*. The experience was quite unnerving, to the point where it became amusing. He later calmed down and we parted company both in agreement that his daughter was a barbarian. This is a characteristic of most hostile parents. If you let them have their say they will burn themselves out and finish the session agreeing with you.

Whenever you see parents and you also need to see their child, it is always best to see the parents first before the child is allowed to join the discussion. This allows frank and open dialogue to take place. Very often the parents may want to speak about how their son or daughter behaves at home. Any matters of a personal nature, which may be relevant to the discussion can be covered. It enables both you and the parents to gain a clearer picture about the issue causing concern. Also, if there is likely to be any adrenaline rush from the parent it is more likely to have diminished by the time the child is asked to join the meeting. It can provide a space in which compromise or negotiation can take place.

You should never allow parents to see another student who may have bearings on the material being discussed. Similarly they must not be given the opportunity to speak to other students on the school premises. I am mindful of an occasion when I asked to see the parents of Charmaine Bracegirdle. Charmaine was a rather precocious Year 9 girl whom students were to name the Monopoly Girl because she was the community chest to the school's Year 11 boys. She was extremely well developed for a 14-year-old and a sharp business acumen too. She spotted the customer potential of her frontage and would charge the lads 50p a feel behind the music block. She was at the point of having earned enough for a deposit on a semi, when she was discovered by an irate head of music, unable to gain access to his music room because of the queue for her services. Her dad was livid and wanted the names and addresses of all her clients, there and then at the meeting. A compromise was reached when I pointed out he and his wife should speak with Charmaine about the ethics and morality of her trade and that speaking with all of her client base would take them at least 12 months.

I would recommend you have all of the necessary paperwork to hand at the meeting. It could be a set of subject reports about the behaviour of a student in lessons. You may have to draw upon witness statements that give an account of an incident that took place concerning the student. These statements should be signed by the witness and also dated. In situations like these it's always best to obtain more than one witness account. Some parents may come to the meeting with a completely different picture about the event. Your job is to present the parents with facts and not opinions. You should try not to be judgemental and always remember to separate the act from the student. Despite all of this, you will still find some mums and dads dispute these facts and apportion blame to someone else. In fact, anyone other than their Gary or Lisa.

I cannot emphasize enough the need to maintain accurate records of incidents concerning students. Some of your year group will have more form than Al Capone. Chronological records of these misdemeanours must be kept in association with their file. I spent a most uncomfortable evening at a pupil's suspension appeal hearing, being turned inside out by a legal representative brought to the meeting by the boy's parents. The woman's gruelling interrogation of the head and myself lasted nearly an hour. I felt she had the ability to secure a blind man a driving license. The important factor that persuaded the governing body to uphold the suspension was the quality of the paperwork supplied by the school. Accurate and ordered records of episodes are extremely important in some of the more unpleasant aspects of the job. If you are a disorganized person in terms of simple administrative tasks, then I would suggest you take a crash course in this area of weakness. It pays dividends!

There may be instances where you feel you need help. Some parents can prove rather troublesome and readily cause you and the school problems. Try to pre-plan these meetings and anticipate any major developments. Your line manager is there to help you and sometimes their expertise is called for. If your line manager is pretty colourless and ineffective, then call upon another member of the leadership group. If you antici-pate you need support, you must get it. Sensitive issues such as child protection necessitates the named person being included.

You will often see parents with the EWO. This is quite a

natural partnership. They will help you do your job more effectively and are the links with specialist help for families.

I would always recommend keeping a record of what was discussed in the meeting. An attending form tutor could be asked to take notes. At the end of the session it is always wise to recap on those notes so that you are both clear about what has been discussed. There may be an agreed action plan formulated at the meeting. There may have been agreed compromise. Decisions such as these are best logged on paper. Should you require a future meeting to discuss any developments such as student progress or changes in domestic arrangements, then agree a date. Confirm this future meeting in writing.

I would recommend setting a time limit on interviews with parents. It should be no longer than half an hour. If either you or they feel that is insufficient then think how long you get with your GP! As you journey towards the end of the time with them, carefully draw the meeting to a close. An easy way of leading into this is to say 'Well, thanks very much for coming up to the school to discuss this matter . . .' Do not suddenly leap up and shake their hand as you are saying this. That is being too abrupt. You are then to recap on what has been discussed during that time and then remind them of any decisions upon which you have both agreed. Then, and only then are you to rise and shake their hand before they go home and you wish you could too.

As you gain more experience in the job you become prepared to meet anything. This includes parents. You will come across over-anxious and often obsessive parents. I recall the parents of a Year 7 boy who was recently diagnosed as an insulin-dependent diabetic. I had explained to his parents the school's response to such a condition in that we had made the medical room available to him for his lunchtime shot. His packed lunch enabled him to eat in accordance with his injection. His lunchtime insulin pen was stored in the office refrigerator. His tutor and teachers were informed and knew the signs of hypoglycaemia and what action to take. His friends too were made aware of the symptoms of low sugar levels and again knew to give him glucose tablets if necessary. His name was on the school medical roll with all of the necessary information in case of emergency.

They would still telephone the school three times a day to check he was well and that he'd given himself his insulin injection. The boy was in complete control of his new disability and became quite embarrassed about the frequent inquiries. He just wanted to play football at break and lunch. The office too, was becoming rather weary over such over-attention. I had the parents in on another two occasions to allay their anxieties. They eventually stopped jamming the school switchboard.

One of the most irritating groups of parents is the pushy parent. This type will try to consume most of your week. Their fundamental aim is, however, quite understandable in that they want the very best for their child. It is just the way they go about achieving this ambition. They are always wanting to come up to the school to see you, a tutor or subject teacher. The headteacher, too, is frequently on their menu. You must be on your guard with such parents. They will remember everything that the school has promised. These parents will complain if ever you or another member of staff fails to meet these assurances. They will not accept poor teaching. They will not accept underachievement. Some pushy parents may, in future meetings, be seen to twist your words. They may falsely claim you have said something. Written records of conversations and action plans are essential with these parents to avoid erroneous accusations. Sometimes pushy parents can either overestimate or even underestimate their child's potential. The true picture needs drawing, with evidence to support the realism. It is with great sadness that I have to admit, teachers are sometimes the quintessential pushy parent.

There will be some parents who openly reveal they cannot cope with the changes that have taken place in their son or daughter during adolescence. They cannot cope with them at home and they sometimes tell you that communication and cooperation has irreversibly broken down. They insist that the behaviour of a 15-year-old today is completely different to a youngster 30 years ago.

In these situations you occasionally act as ACAS between parent and progeny, looking for acceptable compromises. After this free, domestic service has been offered by you, it is then time to address the school issues. However, there are a few parents who refuse to countenance any change of standard and they are the people who continue to experience the antagonism, tetchiness and mood swings from their child.

Some families appear unable to cope with the daily pressures and demands of life. They appear to have given up. There is little organization at home. The family unit appears to have collapsed. The associated problems frequently manifest themselves as attendance, punctuality and welfare issues. You will work in close association with Education Welfare and Social Services in these instances. Solutions to these complex matters are frequently never achieved. You as head of year can help these feckless families by alerting the outside agencies and support services and then work in tandem with them. You make sure other teachers are aware of these difficulties so that irresponsible comments or actions by staff can be avoided.

I was checking the attendance registers early one Monday morning when two grandparents of Patrick, a boy in my year group, appeared at my door. They asked could they see me to discuss something that had happened over the weekend. Patrick sat outside my office while they told me distressing news. A row had ensued between Patrick's parents after a Saturday night out. The heated argument had reached such a pitch that in a moment of hysterical rage and anger the father knifed Patrick's mother. The boy came running from his room only to witness the act. Sadly, Patrick's mother lost consciousness and died as he cuddled her.

The amazing consequence of Patrick having to shoulder such a tragic experience was that he still wanted to come to school on the Monday. School seemed to offer some kind of normality for him. It was somewhere pleasant for him to be, following the appalling event at the weekend. Patrick continued to be courageous for the rest of the time I knew him. Learn to expect anything in this job.

Coping with bereavement and its impact on school is something every head of year should be prepared for. Your mission is to not only provide support for the youngster but also to suggest ways the tutor and members of the tutor group can make coming back to school more bearable. Always write a letter of condolence. It's a personal touch and necessary if the headteacher omits to write one. I would also recommend that you immediately update records on the school roll to avoid letters being sent home incorrectly titled.

Some year heads feel uncomfortable and ill at ease dealing with bereavement and its related problems. I have given special attention to this topic later in the book.

Divorce and separation is also a form of bereavement. Students feel they have lost a mum or a dad. The family is not complete any more. They live with one parent and see the other at prescribed times. The sudden or gradual break-up of a family will certainly impact on school life. You should be vigilant and ask for help from your teaching colleagues in monitoring any possible manifestations. There are certain points you should remember in dealing with the parents of children who are undergoing family change and break-up. Some unpleasant custody cases will seek evidence from you about a student's progress or behaviour in school. You are to present any reasonable request for such information as facts and not opinions and avoid being drawn into the tug-of-love battle. It is also essential to keep both parties informed.

I have been involved in many meetings where I have felt like 'piggy in the middle'. Again, the golden rule in these situations is for you not to take sides. One parent may attempt to score points against the other. Do not make judgements about the situation or attempt to apportion blame on any thing or anybody. If you are seeing parents separately, then it's even more important that you are seen to be neutral. I have heard of some parents using 'the school's opinion' as part of their custody battle. Keep your personal feelings out of any dialogue, for your own sake.

You should ask to be made aware of any decisions made by the courts concerning access. Inform the administrative staff at the school reception of these conditions. Similarly, ensure the contact addresses are correct. If both parents are entitled to being given a school report on their child, then ensure this happens by amending the school administrative records.

A rather irate parent who had been awarded his decree absolute telephoned the school wanting to know why he had not been sent a copy of his daughter's report, while his former wife and her new partner had received a copy two weeks ago! This was very embarrassing for the school and particularly for the head of year answering the phone call.

The majority of parents are fine to work with. Some contacts you have with them will even make you smile. I am reminded of Mr Serafini's wig that would mesmerise staff at parents' evenings. The toupée resembled two layers of shredded wheat resting on his cranium. Each time he would move his head during an emotional conversation about his daughter's progress, the wig would remain stationary, while the rest of his head would move from side to side. One of the first notes I received as a tutor was from a Mrs Blinkhorn. She wrote to explain the absence of her son, Troy. The hurriedly written note read, 'Dear Sir, I am sorry Troy was not at school yesterday cos he was suffering from diar, dyer, dire . . . the shits! I hope this finds you as it leaves me.'

The Parents' Charter embodies the parents' rights and the duty schools have to these parents. You as year manager will oversee and facilitate such partnerships. Remember, schools take on the whole package of the student and their family.

To summarize

1. Make parents feel welcome when they come to the school.
2. Be courteous and try to maintain a pleasant and helpful manner.
3. Listen to what they have to say and try to understand their concerns.
4. It is necessary for you to be patient with some parents. They sometimes take a while to reach their main area of concern.
5. Do not lose your temper.
6. Try to see the parents before the student joins the meeting.
7. Do not let them see other students.
8. Be clear about what you have to say.
9. Have any necessary paperwork at hand.
10. Your account should contain facts and not opinions.
11. Ask a senior member of staff to attend the meeting if you think you'll need help.
12. Make interview notes.
13. Be prepared to make compromises and look for their help and support.
14. Ensure both parties are clear about any action plan you formulate during the meeting.
15. Read back to them the notes from the meeting and set

a date to discuss any future meeting you both feel necessary.

16. Draw the meeting to a close.
17. Remind the parents that should they have any future worries or concerns about anything to do with their son's or daughter's schooling, then they should not hesitate to contact the school.
18. File the interview notes and make relevant staff aware of any important issues.

5 Working alongside teaching colleagues with special responsibilities

Personal and social education was born some 35 years ago. Pastoral staff were the driving force behind its inception. They saw the role the school should play in the personal and social development of its students. Before this time there was little schools did in preparing students for their future lives other than a brief careers interview. I remember my own careers guidance interview conducted by an ageing deputy head, clearly suffering from an acute attack of haemorrhoids at the time. 'Well, you see erm, Carling,' he commenced, getting my name wrong. 'You can get a job inside working with people, or you can get a job outside working without people.' His eyes then opened wide as if he'd had another revelation, or perhaps, another episode of anal discomfort. 'Even the other way around as well! Worth thinking about, erm, Carless,' he concluded. That was it. His meaningful vocational guidance remained with me for years and was to have a profound effect on the rest my life. Not!

There has been a gradual evolution of the contents and implementation of personal and social education. In the early days schools were given a free ticket to develop their own syllabus. In fact there was more help from DFS than the DfES in terms of giving the course content and structure. You were expected to go it alone. We have come a long way in having access to quality resource material. The early days of the uninspiring 'Active Tutorial' booklets, which were about as active as Homer Simpson, have been superseded with more customer-friendly packages, many of which are easy to adapt. The curriculum has been rediscovered, changing its names from PSE (Personal and Social Education), to PSHE (PSE plus Health) and for the moment it exists as PSHCE (PSHE plus Citizenship). The latter takes into account the long-awaited citizenship component that schools had deemed as a crucial inclusion for years. National curriculum and all who are responsible for its ingredients, never cease to surprise me.

Most schools would like to boast a tight and effective programme. It is, however, not so much the nature of their courses I would question, more the delivery of the syllabus contents. Some institutions devolve responsibility for its implementation to form tutors. Others arrange specialist teams of teachers to deliver the goods. Both mechanisms rely on support from outside speakers, videos and worksheets to enhance its presentation. Coordination of either system is down to some member of staff who has often been press-ganged into the job, or brainwashed by a desperate head-teacher anxious to fill the post and then move on to complete their SEF (Self-Evaluation Form).

To many, being a PSHCE coordinator offers about as much kudos and job satisfaction as being responsible for ordering supplies of ketchup in a burger bar. It is to some, the poisoned chalice. Nevertheless, the head of year has to work closely with this friendless soul. The year manager must ensure their tutor team can implement the topic material and that resources are available to them well in advance of the lesson. Ideally, the whole PSHCE package should be there one term in advance. Such organization will give both you and tutors the time to prepare for these lessons.

The head of year should assist the PSHCE coordinator in

any possible training of tutors prior to the lesson. Sadly, because of time issues, this training seldom takes place. Once more, it is the collective responsibility of the pastoral team of year heads to push for this coaching on allocated training days. The degree of assistance a year head can provide becomes more confused if the course is delivered by specialist teams of staff, drawn from different year groups.

If your year group is to be addressed by an outside speaker, then make sure you are there with your tutors to maintain order. Do not allow tutors to slip away or miss the presentation. The success of this area of the school curriculum depends upon its credibility with the punters. If the kids witness an indifferent and jaundiced attitude from its teachers then this apathy will translate to them.

The worst-case scenario, all too common with poorly organized PSHCE managers, is that teaching materials fail to arrive for the start of lessons. Try to help your team by pre-empting these problems and develop a cooperative and supportive relationship with this person, even if you secretly wish to subject them to cyanide.

I have already stressed the value of team teaching with any tutor colleagues who may feel out of their depth with some PSHCE topics. Several years ago, I was helping a young tutor deliver a PSHCE lesson on birth control. Fortunately, we had the family-planning resources kit together with some extremely useful information sheets. We had spoken prior to the lesson and agreed that I would discuss the various methods of contraception and that she would observe the lesson and feel free to supplement the topic. The lesson was off to a good start and the kids showed plenty of maturity and asked sensible questions. We were in the process of discussing condoms and their effectiveness. The young tutor was doing well and she was increasing in confidence. Suddenly, a most pleasant girl, Tina Turner (mother a huge fan) raised her hand with a question. 'Miss, is using a condom safe 'cos I've heard it ain't?' My eager teaching colleague, who was by now bursting with self-assurance, replied, 'Oh, yes Tina, unless there's a prick in it!'

Your middle management counterpart is the head of curriculum area (HOCA). You will have the greatest respect for some, while others you will wonder how they ever achieved promotion. Possibly the loudest moan from heads of year about some members of this group is that they do not do all of their own washing. By this, I mean they readily offload discipline matters to the head of year. This is commonly performed in a rather indirect way. It usually means that members of their department have no confidence in the HOCA's ability to discipline challenging students or in taking the lead when they have to investigate thefts and assaults. You must not allow this to happen. Their job includes running an orderly department and also to support their staff. So, should you receive a visit from a student who bears a note from a maths teacher which reads, 'Come quickly Mr Arkwright, there's trouble at t' mill!' this will usually mean the head of the mathematics department has the discipline skills of Frank Spencer and will be of no use whatsoever.

One head of science I knew was particularly strong at matters concerning behaviour and homework. Any mathematics recidivist would be punished in his twice-weekly detention sessions. He would subject his clientele to solving mathematical problems while he played Harry Secombe and Bing Crosby vinyls. The kids would groan in agony and vow never to forget their homework again. The same chap was very much anti-Ofsted and when he was asked to show an inspector evidence of departmental record keeping, he showed the grey-suited assassin his complete collection of Val Doonican LPs. I would not recommend such defiance.

Another example of heads of department running their own shop was revealed to me when I was trawling through a student's behaviour report. I had been at the school a couple of months and did not know all of the staff. I noticed that he had several poor comments from various departments but never one from history. 'Who takes you for history Sam?' I inquired. Sam, the miscreant, replied, 'Mrs Charalambou, sir.' Doris Charalambou was in charge of history and was a respected head of department. If she said it was Tuesday to the kids, it was Tuesday! I followed his response with, 'Why don't you get bad behaviour comments from her?' Sam paused for a moment and seemed surprised at my innocence. 'She's a psycho, Sir. Nobody messes her about!'

A duty usually undertaken by one of your tutors is to collate set work for students with a long-term illness, or a student who has been given the red card and is excluded from school. An aide-mémoire is usually sent to all of the student's teachers asking for some work to be set. This request is frequently reinforced by putting another written plea on the staffroom notice board. Another mechanism for ensuring this appeal registers with these teachers is to announce it at a staff briefing, or its equivalent. It is with great sadness that I have to report a noticeable lack of success with some departments. There are certain colleagues who suffer amnesia when it comes to uncomplicated chores such as these. It is your role as year manager to intervene in these situations and to stress the urgency of the matter to both subject teacher and their head of department. You will drown in a sea of excuses, but stick to your guns and insist the work is provided on that day.

I recall one head of technology whose procrastination with any aspect of life was obvious to all. Ironically, he reminded the world of this fact when he placed a notice on a door in the technology corridor which requested students not to run. The notice read, 'SLOW HEAD of DEPARTMENT'.

Heads of subject will sometimes request to see parents of students. I feel it wise that they should inform you or the pupil's tutor of this intention. It may be they are unaware of certain circumstances relating to the child's behaviour or work. There should be a protocol in the school which secures such procedure. If there is not, then I would consult your fellow year heads and move for its introduction. It prevents any possible embarrassing or uncomfortable meetings. Communication in both directions is so important.

You may find you are drawn into a situation involving the student, the parents and the head of department. Frequently, your job is to act as an arbitrator. This calls on your people skills to look for a solution or compromise between two intransigent parties. The knack here is to steer the debate in such a way that at the end of the meeting both sides feel they have aired their views and achieved something positive.

The aim is to work in harmony with heads of curriculum areas and foster a mutually supportive culture. However, I am once more reminded of a quote from my uncle Horace who would say, 'There's nowt as queer as folk, lad!' This expression, which miraculously on this occasion did not concern itself with micturition, simply implied that all people are different and they will behave in ways different to you. Expect anything.

A person with whom you will have many dealings is the SENCo (Special Educational Needs Coordinator). If you haven't had much to do with them before, then you must understand the nature of their job. The two of you need to have a positive relationship so that the students in your charge with individual needs will benefit. Broadly speaking, their task is to raise the achievement of children with special educational needs. They oversee the day-to-day operation of the school's SEN (Special Educational Needs) policy and constantly liaise with and advise fellow teachers. You will be one of these contacts. They will provide you with the information you require to see the complete picture of the children with individual needs in your year group. It is important for this information to be relayed to you by the SENCo because you too will have to deal with issues relevant to these needs. Contrary to the thoughts of a minority of year heads, you have a shared responsibility for the progress and happiness of these children. The minefield of inclusion frequently creates tension between the SENCo, parents and the classroom teacher. The head of year acts as a mediator in these instances and your personal skills will be taxed to bring about some form of agreement and reconciliation.

Some schools are fortunate enough to have a team of SEN teachers. The majority of our institutions have a SENCo who works with a band of learning support/teaching assistants (LSAs and TAs). Just as your fellow teaching colleagues have variable attributes, so too have the LSAs. Just as keeping on the right side of the most powerful person in the school, the caretaker, helps you make progress with your job, so too would I advise you have a good relationship with this group. They see life at the chalk-face and give you all kinds of information.

SENCos keep all of the necessary information about the children in your year with SEN. This vital data will include statements of special educational needs together with paperwork bearing acronyms such as BSP (Behaviour Support Plan) and IEP (Individual Education Plan). You will soon absorb these ciphers into your daily vocabulary. You should be quite clear what this documentation prescribes.

From time to time you may be required to attend consultation sessions with parents together with the SENCo and the educational psychologist. Statemented students will require an annual review and the SENCo will remind you of its imminence. ARs (Annual Reviews) deemed to be straightforward will probably not require your presence. I can recall several ARs over the years when these meetings were solely attended by the SENCo. However, if the progress of the student is giving cause for concern, then I feel it is essential you attend. You will be there in a supportive role for the SENCo and it also gives you a chance to inject some classroom realism into the proceedings.

The SENCo should have in-depth knowledge of any organic or psychological problem experienced by a student in your year. You will learn from them about the nature of the condition. Again, try to develop a good working relationship with this member of staff. As head of year you will not be expected to be an authority on autistic spectrum disorder or know detailed cytogenetics of Down's syndrome. The SENCo will discuss an outline of the condition and stress the specific needs of these students. SENCos will frequently provide in-service training for you, the tutor and staff who teach this student. This is particularly important with students who show problems with behaviour and concentration in lessons. The SENCo should be the person who can suggest possible strategies to enable staff to deal with the problems generated by these pupils. Similarly, the SENCo will enlighten staff about any organic disabilities suffered by certain students and provide information about what to do in particular circumstances. I remember a teacher claiming they had not been told of a pupil's enuresis, despite receiving numerous notices about the condition. This member of staff refused to allow the student leave to visit the loo half-way through a SATs practice test. The classroom floor became Lake Windermere and a teaching colleague persuaded the teacher to purchase *The Times Educational Supplement* the following Friday.

You will also work closely with the SENCo if outside agencies are involved with a student in your charge. Such input may come from the educational psychologist, social services, the local health authority and voluntary bodies.

If a student in your year is recommended for a statutory assessment, this means there is to be a detailed investigation to find out the child's special educational needs and what specific help that child requires. If an assessment is granted so that a statement of special educational needs can be assembled, this process takes a long time. It is a frustrating and protracted period of time waiting for the production of an agreed statement. The process takes up to six months, and the child may move from your year group into the next. It is important that year managers understand the funding mechanisms associated with SEN and what entitlement means in terms of hard cash, resource and staffing issues.

You must know the students in your year with these individual needs. The statemented and ESOL (English for speakers of other languages) students together with those who are openly recognized as EBD (emotionally and behaviourally disturbed) will be the first drawn to your attention. However, there will also be students for whom there has been no statutory assessment. You must be aware of students with a marked aptitude, the able, gifted and talented. These students are easily overlooked because, in general, they cause fewer obvious problems. Any extension work programme for them should come through the SENCo and heads of curriculum area. Please do not forget, too, those students who clearly struggle with mainstream and have been denied a statement. Sometimes a 'notice in lieu' is issued by the decision panel and the school itself has to provide the future support for these children. This often places unacceptable demands on the SENCo, you and the child's subject teachers. Those students who are not statemented and yet are clearly emotionally and behaviourally disturbed will consume much of your time. Staff will frequently look to you and the SENCo for supplying magic formulae for dealing with these challenging pupils.

You may have students who are in the care of the Local Authority (LA), or students with social problems. It may be that liaison with special needs is a part of their support package. Special needs today is indeed a hazardous area and one that embraces a broad spectrum of students. An implicit part of your role as head of year will, therefore, necessitate cooperative and purposeful work with the SENCo.

If you take your year group through from Year 7 to Year 11, you will need to work with someone who is in charge of work experience and also deals with careers guidance. There has been considerable change in DfES recommendations for a planned programme of careers education. They now insist that careers education should start as early as Year 7, so that by the end of Year 9, students are better prepared to make their first set of decisions. These are the choices that will, in part, influence their lives at Key Stage 4 and beyond. During this time the teacher who has responsibility for the careers programme will need help from you and your tutor team to cover the groundwork enabling the students to successfully manage this key transition stage. The Connexions support and advisory team will play a greater role at Key Stage 4 and beyond. They enable teenagers to learn about jobs and careers, as well as providing them with information on topics such as money matters, relationships, equal opportunities, housing and benefits, drugs and people's basic rights. Personal Advisers (PAs) are the personnel who deliver elements of this package. PAs are frequently the old Careers Adviser with new clothes, new training and bigger briefcases.

Information must flow between you and the teacher with responsibility for careers education. You must know what he/she is recommending for the youngsters in your year and you must provide any relevant background information for them. The jigsaw pieces of this guidance programme must fit together in a realistic way and be student-focused.

Your school 'work experience' programme will either take place in Year 10 or in the early days of Year 11. The mechanism for selecting this work will be governed by the school having its own employer database, or one provided by agencies such as Trident. Most common is a mixture of placements privately arranged by the students themselves, some from school contacts and the rest from the work-placement agency.

Work with the member of staff in charge of work experience. You know the year group with its potential problems, the work experience coordinator may not. You are able to predict the pupils who will have problems with the selection process. Insist, as far as is possible, the job list of the year group is complete at least a week in advance of the work experience commencement date. This allows you to deal with the apathetic and work phobic. By this, I am referring to students and not your colleagues. Pay particular attention to the students with special needs and see if the pupil and their parents are happy with the placements.

Some students may find job descriptions difficult to decipher. I remember one lad from Stepney who thought the term 'manual labour' on his job sheet was a citizen of Barcelona. Another point of confusion arose when a parent thought a job description reading: 'The student will be working with Microsoft Windows', was a reference to a double-glazing firm in Hoxton.

It is the teacher in charge of work experience who must ensure the work-placement database is accurate and up to date. Some employers come off this register due to bad experiences with students. I recall one garage proprietor releasing a Year 11 student who had been a petrol pump attendant for only 15 minutes. He was caught giving free petrol to ten of his mates on their 50cc motorbikes.

There is one fundamental piece of advice I must give to all heads of year as they deal with colleagues who make decisions concerning the students in your charge. Always ask them to put the agreed recommendation in writing. A decision made during a conversation over a hastily quaffed coffee at morning break will not suffice. This may seem an unimportant and trivial recommendation to the uninitiated but to seasoned campaigners it is a golden rule. It prevents two possibilities. First, they can't say they never agreed to that. Second, when they do commit the accord to paper it reminds them about any action that must be taken and there is more chance of it happening. Remember, staff will cause you more problems than the kids!

To summarize

1. Develop a good working relationship with the PSHCE coordinator, even though you may frequently contemplate homicide.
2. Ask them for the PSHCE syllabus, together with resource material, at least a term in advance.
3. Ensure your tutors attend any PSHCE training, and do not allow them to 'bunk off' presentations delivered to their tutor group by outside speakers.
4. Try team teaching some PSHCE topics with certain tutors.
5. Try to establish a positive working attitude with HOCAs, even though you may once more consider homicide.
6. Do not shoulder the disciplinary responsibilities of HOCAs. Let them sort out their own shop.
7. Insist and ensure that work is set by teachers of excluded or long-term absent pupils.
8. Make certain heads of subject are fully briefed on the full picture of a student before they request to see parents.
9. Be prepared to act as arbitrator at potentially difficult meetings between HOCA and parents. This should be an exception rather than a rule.
10. Forge a good working relationship with the SENCo. Again, at times, thoughts of homicide should not be excluded.
11. Make sure you know all of the necessary information

concerning students with special educational needs in your year group.

12. Use the SENCo to help to formulate an action plan for non-statemented yet needy students, who struggle with mainstream education.

13. Talk to those LSAs and TAs you trust about what goes on in the classroom.

14. Push for statements of special needs to be made on students who you and the SENCo feel have been overlooked.

15. Attend annual review meetings that could be problematic.

16. Push for staff training on ways of dealing with students whose behaviour, because of the nature of their special needs, will cause their teachers problems.

17. Provide any relevant information on students for staff who are responsible for careers guidance and work experience.

18. Always insist decisions made by staff about matters concerning students are put in writing.

6 Working with support agencies

I worked for many years as head of house at a large boys'
comprehensive school in inner London. There was a rough,
tough and macho atmosphere in the corridors and play-
grounds. Kate Adie and Rageh Omar were employed as
lunchtime supervisors and would frequently report on the
trouble spots around the school. The place was held together
by a tight pastoral system in the form of vertically arranged
tutor groups within a house system. Each tutor group therefore had equal numbers of students from Years 7 to 10. Year 11
students had their own separate tutor groups within the
house. I must admit to having initial reservations about
working within such a framework. My previous contact with
pastoral systems had been with horizontal year structures.
However, I soon began to enjoy the breadth of experience it
gave me being able to work with students across the secondary school age range.

It was a typical inner-city school with its associated attendance, behaviour and social problems. That was just with the
staff! Similar difficulties too were representative of its student
clientele.

I was anxious to do well and to make a success of my first
real taste of pastoral responsibility. I had so much energy,

enthusiasm and determination. I was, however, mindful of something told me by a year head for whom I had the greatest of respect. He stressed that heads of year new to the post should not allow the job to run away with them. They should know their professional boundaries, and be ready to seek help from support agencies whenever necessary. Sometimes, freshly appointed year managers feel they should be able to solve problems and get results all on their own. They feel it is a sign of weakness if they summon reinforcements or assistance. This is far from the truth. Being able to judge when a situation calls for specialist help, and when this help leads to a satisfactory conclusion, is a sign of sound judgement and a professional approach to the job.

Schools today have a number of specialist support agencies with whom they can collaborate. These will include the Education Welfare Service, the Schools' Psychological Service, the Area Health Authority, Social Services and the police. All will have areas of expertise on which you can call. The skill is knowing when and in what capacity these agencies can be called upon to assist you the head of year, the students and their families. These support bodies will expect from you or the headteacher, documented evidence of the school's concerns and any previous action taken. This chronological account is really your responsibility. You will incur the wrath of the camp commandant if this paperwork is vague and incomplete. Once more I stress the importance of keeping up-to-date and accurate records. You should be like Caesar's wife and beyond reproach in maintaining details of correspondence, data, reports and agreed action plans.

The service with which you will have greatest contact is Education Welfare. The Education Welfare Officer (EWO), or Education Social Workers as they are sometimes called, should act as an extra pair of hands in helping you deal with a number of issues. Not all of these will include attendance and punctuality. Just as the EWO must be clear about the school's responsibilities concerning the children in their charge, so too must you as year head understand the nature of the support they can offer the school.

The initial duty of an EWO is to check through the tutor group attendance registers in your year group. They will act as a second pair of eyes and uncover any unexplained absences you have overlooked. They should also highlight any patterns of absences worth investigating. EWOs follow up any irregular attendances and check these patterns are not worsening. Do not leave such analysis to them. It is your responsibility to stay on top of attendance concerns. The EWO should bring such anomalies to your attention on rare occasions. Their remit is to respond to referrals of pupils with levels of unacceptable school attendance. The head of year will have produced an agenda including such concerns prior to your meeting. Students who feature on this list will have been discussed by you and the tutor.

The EWO may be asked to produce a report on attendance for the headteacher or the school's governing body. Education Welfare may be asked to run training workshops for school teaching and administrative staff on attendance matters and registration practice. The EWO works within the framework of the law and upholds the school's attendance policy. It is Education Welfare who initiates any legal proceedings against parents who fail to ensure their child attends school regularly. Some parents do not accept this responsibility. Some will even refuse to discuss ways of improving their child's attendance. The EWO has to be actively involved in such instances. Their role is not only to be seen working in partnership with the school but also to enforce the law of the land.

Excuses supplied by some parents for their child's poor attendance are sometimes easy to X-ray. I recall one parent who ran a market stall, whose 14-year-old son had frequent absences on Wednesdays and Fridays (market days). The non-attendance suddenly stopped at those times when one Wednesday lunchtime the EWO and I bought a pound of plums from the boy on his dad's stall. The EWO dutifully requested the father's presence at an attendance review meeting and threats of legal proceedings and fines produced a healthier attendance record.

Condoned absences like these are becoming an increasing problem and you certainly need the help of EWS in dealing with them. Parents who frequently keep their children away from school because of repeated bouts of illness need reminding by the EWO that medical certificates will need to be produced explaining the nature of their debility. This request can often bring about a miraculous improvement in their fettle and attendance statistics.

If students are away from school for a protracted period of time with acceptable reasons, then your EWO can arrange home tuition. Pupils recovering from an operation or those who are likely to be in hospital for some time will fall into this category. This will also involve a lot of footwork for you and the tutor in collating syllabus material and schemes of work for the home tutor. Such preparation tasks should facilitate relevant and appropriate tuition so that the student does not fall behind with their studies. Education Welfare will work in close cooperation with pregnant teenagers and teenage mothers enabling them to continue with their education.

Pupils who have been excluded from school either on a fixed-term or permanent basis will need to continue with their education. This process will involve the assistance of the EWO and again, much time-consuming collection of set work from HOCAs by you and the tutor. You will liaise with Education Welfare in developing strategies for avoiding exclusions of pupils. Students who continuously cause the school problems will need to have experienced approved remedial programmes for the possibility of a permanent exclusion to show any likelihood of being upheld by governing bodies.

Education Welfare will supply information to a child and their family on child employment issues. Many students will want part-time jobs to supplement either their own or their family's income. EWS will need to know factors such as the nature of the employment, conditions of service and health and safety issues. They will have information on the number of hours per day and week a student is able to work. Relevant work permits or certificates of employment can then be issued to the employer, the child and their family. Despite this mechanism being in place you will discover many of your students who are in employment without such authorization being in place.

I was informed by one of my tutors of a girl in her tutor group, whose punctuality for school was now becoming a cause for concern. The girl looked pale and was reported to have fallen asleep in physics and food technology lessons. Knowing the teachers of these subjects, I could well understand her drifting into the arms of Morpheus. However, when I saw the girl it transpired she had recently acquired a job as waiter in a restaurant and was working long evening and weekend hours. The number of hours she did was way in excess of those permitted for her age. The girl's father had recently become unemployed and she had taken the decision get a job to help with home finances. The EWO helped by informing the restaurant proprietor and the family of their legal obligation and responsibilities and that the school would be monitoring the girl's progress. The girl's punctuality improved, as well as reducing her coma potential in encounters with physics and food technology.

Your year group may contain a thespian or two. The proud parents of the starlet to be may write to the school requesting time away to perform. This may be to allow their precocious progeny to either model children's thermal underwear for a catalogue or be in the chorus of Dante's Inferno on Ice. The headteacher will consult you on this one before he/she makes a judgement. Your EWO too will need to be briefed.

In the course of your tenured position as head of year you will encounter child-protection issues. The EWO should work in close association with you through these difficult waters. Other agencies will also demand an input into these circumstances. It is sometimes the case that investigative work undertaken by your EWO will uncover problems of this nature. A home visit carried out by an EWO at the request of the year head may reveal domestic disorder and feckless parents who clearly neglect their children. The visit could also highlight poverty issues and the subsequent need for clothing allowances and free school meals. You will have a diary distended with meetings and appointments but I would suggest you attend the occasional home visit in the company of an EWO to see parents who have proved difficult to contact. These visits will frequently open your eyes as to what the child has to shoulder and to witness in their home life. It may help in you understanding the full picture of that student.

Some schools may have an EWO on site. In many schools year heads will see their EWOs once a week, and unfortunately others less frequently. If you have a good working relationship with an EWO, and the EWO turns up to these timetabled meetings, it will allow you to do your job of running the year group more effectively. I have worked with EWOs whom I can rely upon, and who know exactly what they can do to assist me with my caseload. I have also tried to cope in situations where I feel I'm working at a problem on my own because an EWO has missed a chain of scheduled appointments. At one time there seemed to be a multitude of vacancies for EWOs and many of my counterparts did sense they were working in isolation. Alternatively, it may be that you feel you are just getting to know an EWO and you are working well together when they will leave. I once had three

EWOs in a year. Was it my socks or what? Whatever it was, such circumstances precipitated a lack of continuity in dealing with important ongoing issues and led to some unsatisfactory conclusions.

You must, however, remember that EWOs have other personnel in other schools with whom they work. Like you, they too will have an expanding caseload and have a difficult job to do. It is important that you respect the guidelines within which they must operate and the prescribed levels of intervention. The EWS can provide an essential link between schools and other support services. The assistance and contacts they provide enable you as head of year to be more successful in managing your caseload.

One agency you will discover, usually through the SENCo, is the Schools' Psychological Service (SPS). The Educational Psychologist (EP) is someone you may see around the school on one of their rationed visits. You may get a chance to speak with this busy soul when the individual education plan (IEP) for a student hits problems. IEPs are drafted by the SENCo when a student's teachers have significant concerns about their behaviour or progress. You will also have a significant role to play because you will have been on the receiving end of complaints and concerns expressed by these teachers.

The IEP will have to indentify the targets the school will work towards with that child. The SENCo will report back to you on any progress made by the student with these targets. Like all targets set for students, they should be viewed as realistic and achievable. Under normal circumstances, you will usually find that the SENCo does not need to report back with a summary of progress. You will already have sensed developments when teachers offload to you at the earliest opportunity.

The lack of improvement of the student will often demand the SENCo seeking professional advice from the school's link

EP. Parents continue to be informed of this process, and the SENCo will ask the parents to agree to their child having a consultation session with the EP. They will also advise parents that there will be an opportunity for them to be involved in this consultation meeting. Some parents will not countenance the involvement of an EP with their child. They may refuse to see the complete picture. There are parents who feel uneasy about their child's involvement with an EP, and that there is a certain stigma associated with such consultation. You have serious problems if this happens. If the difficulties are rooted in the poor behaviour of the student, there sometimes follows unpleasantness from the parents about any disciplinary sanctions the school is prepared to use. Anticipate the classic accusation that their child is being picked on by the teachers.

The way to avoid such antagonism is for you and the SENCo to have paved the way for such involvement in a diplomatic, tactful yet purposeful way. You could even say that enlisting the help of the EP may be a way of reducing the possibility of future exclusions. Stress the word 'may' and do not put it in writing.

The outcome of any EP consultation is to find a practical way forward. They may recommend building on any approach that has already met with some success. They can suggest trying out different strategies. Often they will request more information to get a better idea of the nature of the problem. This could be by enlisting the help of fellow professionals such as the GP or a member of the specialist teaching services. Occasionally a more detailed assessment by the EP is requested. Any action plan suggested by the EP will be kept on record and a copy sent to the child's parents.

I have witnessed a broad range of EP recommendations over the years as varied as arranging sessions with a worker from Education Guidance to making provision for a student to attend an adolescent unit at one of the major London teaching hospitals. Frequently their prescription is to allow the school to manage the problem and suggest some ways forward to help. If you don't understand about specific learning difficulties such as dyslexia, then I would suggest as head of year you should familiarize yourself with these issues.

The archetypal EP is softly spoken, unflappable, pensive and appears in need of some psychological support himself. You will share the same opinion as the SENCo in that there are never enough allocated slots for EP involvement in the school's calendar. The EP is, however, an essential link person for helping schools manage those youngsters who have the most significant and complex learning difficulties.

The pupil referral service (PRS) provides a means of providing some respite for certain students who find the pressures of school life to be too much. These students are likely to have experienced behavioural problems, but not all. The PRS gives these students an opportunity to be away from the daily demands of their school and gives the teachers at the pupil referral unit some time to put into practice strategies which may help in the successful full-time reintegration of the student back into mainstream education. A dual registration mechanism is employed, since the student remains on the school roll while they attend sessions at the PRU (Pupil Referral Unit).

The school can recommend a student for consideration for a place at the PRU. You will be involved in facilitating this placement. You should work with the EWO, headteacher or their deputy in arranging the consideration process. There are a limited number of places at one of these establishments and even though staff will tell you they teach a class with 25 eligible candidates from your year group, that's hard luck. Placements usually come about due to a catalogue of problems, some of which may have already resulted in temporary exclusions. A decision made by a member of the PRU will result in some one-to-one counselling sessions taking place in school, or placement at the unit on a part- or full-time basis.

The aim is to formulate and test different support procedures that will be of use to teachers. The idea is to bring about successful reintegration of the student and avoid such sanctions as permanent exclusion.

I always feel it takes a certain breed of person to work at a PRU. I worked at such a centre in a depressed area of north London. It was housed in a gloomy basement of a public building. Pupil numbers were small and there were very few resources available to us. Lessons were no more than 40 minutes, there were good, trouble-free days but it was rather like working in a gelignite factory. It would only take a change in mood from one student to light the touchpaper of the rest. The few staff who worked there all smoked furiously during their non-contact time and the head of the unit was a regular subscriber to Diazepam Weekly. Many positive things were achieved with the students at the centre, but when a situation kicked off, it could be quite alarming for anyone visiting the place for the first time. I admire and have the greatest of respect for staff who work at PRUs. They can, however, be sometimes guilty of expecting an improvement shown by a student at the centre, with its small-scale and informal atmosphere, to transfer to mainstream schooling.

Your only involvement with the area health authority may come through contact with the school nurse. Today their brief forms part of the tapestry of the healthy schools programme. They have a general overview of the health of students. They will offer clinics on diet and weight watching, as well as giving advice on contraception and sexually transmitted infections. You should value their input at case conferences, because some kids see them as a resource set apart from the school and will often talk freely about problems they may be experiencing. Gone are the days of the 'Nit Nurse' who gave kids a scrape with a fine-tooth comb and followed this with a dollop of cod-liver oil. Their brief has fortunately widened to offer counselling and advice to students. I did work with a family, all of whose children went through my charge. They were the Hill family whose commitment to personal hygiene was on the same level as a skunk. The four kids, Dean, Debbie, Zak and young Keanu in Year 7 all stank and persistently suffered from head lice. The school nurse referred to them as the Von Trapp family from *The Sound of Music*. She would sing in the staff room, 'The Hills are alive . . .!' She was very good with the kids and they liked her. They would call her the Angel of the North, not because she was a nurse from North Shields, but because she was 18 stone in weight and 6 feet 4 tall.

The police School's Liaison Officer (SLO) can sometimes have an office on the school premises. They work with the Community Link Officer and know what there is to know about the local area from which the majority of the school's population is drawn. They can supply you with background information on matters as wide-ranging as which of your year they have found skinning up behind the local shops, to who has just been collared for TDA (taking and driving away a motor vehicle). SLOs will readily give you advice about new activities of your youngsters and their mates in the community. I recollect them being very helpful to the school and parents when the glue-sniffing craze seemed endemic in the 80s. I remember being able to reciprocate this help when a consignment of trainers was knocked off on the Caledonian Road. I was delivering a PSE lesson to my Year 9 group and noticed they were all kitted out in new and dazzling white trainers. Sussed!

SLOs are ready to help with the school and year assembly programmes. The delivery of parts of the citizenship syllabus will fall within their remit. They will run workshops for youngsters and parents. They will often assist the EWO with truancy patrols. They should be consulted on matters relating to theft and assault if the need arises. They may have made a contribution to formulating the school drugs policy. They are yet another support body with whom the head of year will work.

You may come into contact with Social Services in a number of ways. They may be working with the families of the students you teach to help with one of many possible issues. It could be to help a family where there is chronic sickness at home. They provide help to families where there is domestic violence. In general they assist families where there is helplessness or a breakdown in the family unit. Social Services will liaise with you if any of your students are in the care of the local authority. Key workers will be appointed to support and oversee these individuals or family groups. They too act as facilitators able to enlist the input of specialist help agencies.

Child-protection issues will instantly demand their attention. A social worker is just one of the personnel along with the police and EWO who will pursue child-protection issues. The caseload of social workers is immense and like their colleagues in Education Welfare, they always seem understaffed. I have always found working with Social Services a frustrating experience. I have waited up to six hours for a social worker to turn up in an urgent child-protection matter and I have witnessed children taken off the 'At Risk Register' when there were still unresolved areas of concern. Expect anything.

Something that seems common to all of the support agencies is that they never seem to see the same urgency as you in dealing with matters. You may feel they achieve some things in weeks that you feel could have been sorted in hours.

To summarize

1. Do not try to achieve everything on your own. Be prepared to enlist the help of the support agencies.

2. Know your professional boundaries and request their expertise.

3. Consult a fellow year head or your line manager if you are uncertain about asking for this help.

4. Always think of the worst-case scenario if you do not request their input.

5. Keep documented evidence and a chronological history of events for the open scrutiny of the support bodies. Ensure this information is accurate.

6. Keep on top of attendance in your year. Scrutinize the registers as frequently as possible. Look for patterns of non-attendance that your tutors may have missed. Act swiftly in truancy cases.

7. Never miss a scheduled appointment with the EWO.

8. Be prepared to accompany the EWO on a home visit in certain instances.

9. Ensure work is set by subject teachers for students who are long-term sick or those students who are excluded.

10. Know the students in your year who undertake part-time employment. Inform the EWO of these students.

11. Know the students who are involved in some way with Social Services. Ask the key worker if there's anything the school should know.

12. Know the students in your care who receive free school meals or clothing allowances.

13. Know the contents of the IEPs of any student in your year.

14. Be prepared to attend ARs of students in certain instances.

15. Do not forget students in your year who attend the PRU. Visit them from time to time and take an interest in their progress even though you may feel relieved they are there!

16. Have your paperwork complete if you intend to recommend students for the PRU.

17. Keep on good terms with the school nurse. She may be able to make you understand a student in greater depth.

18. Keep on good terms with the SLO, and make them feel welcome when they come into the school. You never know when you may need their assistance!

7 Dealing with conflict

There were some big lads in Year 11. Some produced more testosterone than Mike Tyson, some looked as though they started shaving when they were a foetus. I was a Year 11 tutor, and my year manager was Mick Jarris. His full name was Hugh Michael Jarris but preferred to use the first name Michael for obvious reasons.

There was a knock at the staffroom door. It was one of those knocks that signified impending doom. A trembling, yet excited Year 8 pupil garbled the alarm to a teacher who was currently consuming a mug of tea while simultaneously chomping on a mouthful of chocolate digestives.

'Can you tell Mr Jarris Year 11s are havin' a riot in the canteen!' The teacher on the receiving end of this message relayed the information to Mick, who was on the opposite side of the room. The unflappable year head calmly walked out of the room while staff seated nearest the door fished fragments of chocolate digestive from their break-time coffee.

I decided to accompany him so that I could see him in action. He still appeared unruffled even as he opened the door of the dining area. There was mayhem, with tables, chairs and students scattered across the room. He appeared not to be alarmed by the scene before him. He momentarily paused and then acted decisively.

'Right!' he commanded, in a loud voice. The melée stopped. He then pointed towards several clusters of students. 'You lot put those tables back! You lot sort those chairs out! You lot get this mess tidied! And you, get your tie on!' He then walked through the pacified crowd, which parted like the Red Sea for Moses. I've never seen such control. He then announced, 'I want to see you, you, you and you. Now! You go over there! You there! You in that corner and you outside my room!' He chose his sample well, for this motley crew of narks would guarantee him all the information he required.

I was most impressed with the confident and authoritative way he dealt with the situation. He seemed unaffected by my compliments and admiration. He was very brief in his response. 'Listen Brian,' he said in his customary softly spoken way, 'I took my time going down to the room because I was thinking about what I may find and how I would handle the problem when I got there. You've got to think things through and not just jump in with both feet. When I opened the door I was scared stiff but you must give a confident air that shows you are in control. The kids expect it from you.'

I learned my trade as head of year over a period of many years. One aspect of the job I quickly mastered was to be able to deal effectively with conflict. You will employ this skill on a daily basis. There are certain ways of bringing about a successful conclusion to these taxing and stressful situations. You will acquire this expertise by learning from the mistakes you will make or by observing colleagues whose modus operandi gets the desired result.

Confrontation will cut across your path in a number of ways. A teaching colleague may not handle a disagreement with a student too well. They seem to press all of the wrong buttons in their attempt at managing the dispute. The situation soon deteriorates as both parties allow their adrenaline to flow to such a degree that any faint chance of reconciliation and cooperation quickly sails out of the window, occasionally accompanied by a chair. You will have to cope with angry parents who appear unable to see any link between wood and trees. You will most certainly work in an antithetical way to Frank Warren by defusing tension between two pugilistic students. There will also be instances when you act as peacemaker should a member of the public see fault with student behaviour. In all of these minefields there are some things you should and should not do.

In any confrontation, never lose control, even if the person with whom you are attempting a conversation is re-enacting the eruption of Krakatoa. You will look as foolish as your volcanic partner and forfeit any chance of a settlement. Be careful with the pitch and tone of your voice, any excess will promote tension. If you keep your cool you have more chance achieving the desired result. Remember Gunga Din! Be careful about eye contact and your general body language. Piercing eye contact appears rather threatening, and the arms-folded stance is interpreted as a defensive and intractable response. Personal space is also an important ingredient in any meeting. If you are in their face and covering them with saliva there is obviously a problem, and any conversation will certainly not take a turn for the better.

If you are required to attempt a settlement between a teacher and a pupil, both parties will want you to support them. I would suggest you see the teacher and the student separately before any joint meeting so you can gather the facts and also undertake some research work. This detective work may be to see other students or by asking a head of department about any previous discord. When you see them separately give them both the impression you are there in a supportive role. You are becoming involved to help the situation and to attempt to find a solution. This foundation work will settle the antagonists and allow them to feel progress is being made. It may be the teacher or the student was having a particularly bad day. It may have been the language used by either party that caused the Semtex to go off. Your mission, therefore, is to find the real reason for the altercation. Always bear in mind what may happen if this contretemps is unsatisfactorily resolved. The pupil will involve parents, the teacher may involve the senior management or a trade union. This may sound far-fetched but it is sensible to have all of your paperwork intact. This will include an incident report form completed by the teacher, witness statements and the student statement. Any other potentially useful intelligence you have gathered should also be retained.

If you are summoned to deal with an acrimonious exchange between these two sections of the school community, take the immediate tension out of the situation by asking the student to wait outside your room and then ask the teacher to give you a few moments when they have calmed down. There's very little point in trying to proceed when both factions are still highly charged. If the teacher raises any objections to you asking for witness statements then it is worth pointing out to them it's in their own interest for this to happen.

Once both have restored control of their nervous systems you can proceed in gathering an honest and accurate account of the incident and anything that may have precipitated the confrontation. At the same time reassure both student and teacher the matter will be thoroughly investigated and action taken.

The pieces of the jigsaw will slowly come together and your job is to follow the school's discipline policy and any procedures it recommends. If it appears the student has clearly been responsible for the conflict then the path you should follow is relatively uncomplicated. Any discipline sanctions should be invoked and the student made to apologize to the member of staff. If the student is a regular offender then they should be placed on report to monitor their behaviour, as well as suggesting strategies to control their aggression. Clearly document any behaviour support plans and enlist the cooperation of the parents.

The more difficult task is when the teacher was clearly responsible for causing the engagement. They must be made to see it was their behaviour that created the problem. Suggest ways of dealing with similar situations that will secure better results. Some staff and students have short fuses and they need to work on this anger control. Suggest some ways this can be achieved.

If they have upset the student then they too should apologize. Ensure the head of department is aware of the incident. If it is the head of department who is the offending person, then they should know better. Monitor any further developments and look for any patterns. Incidents involving confrontations in the classroom should be handled by the head of subject. On occasions you will be summoned in their absence, or as the duty teacher 'on call'.

If the situation involves a senior member of staff with either status in the school or in terms of years served in the job, there is a tendency for them to expect you always to support their behaviour. If you pick up vibes that show they were wrong to respond in such a way then do not hesitate in telling them this. Some senior staff will try to coerce your support. Stick to your guns and pursue the legitimate course of action. I had the misfortune to work with a head of faculty with some 30 years of teaching under his belt. He was a dreadful chap who hated kids so much he would refer to them as insurgents. He was once seen by a junior member of staff in the loo swigging some Irish malt before going to teach period three. 'You must face your audience with confidence dear boy!' he advised. This was his formula for addressing the dimension of teaching and learning. He then adjusted his spectacles, passed a loud shaft of flatus and proceeded to cause yet more problems. He was a constant source of work and irritation for all heads of year.

You may be summoned to deliver a verbal admonishment to a class consisting of some of your year group. If it's a crisis and the teacher needs immediate help, then you are justified in intervening and dealing with the trouble. Be careful when you do this not to humiliate the teacher by some of the things you say. You can enter a classroom and encounter what a friend of mine calls 'anti-gravity teaching'. This is where the kids fail to respond to the laws of physics and are crawling up the walls and across the ceiling. Restoring order should be carried out in a way that includes the teacher, and one which indicates both support and partnership.

It is wise to use similar techniques when you need to resolve conflict between angry students. If it's a fight, you may be unlucky enough to be in the vicinity. When the fight has been arrested and the two combatants separated, you should keep one with you and send the other to wait outside your office. Do not send them off together because they may 'kick off' again in another part of the school. You should not attempt to question these students in front of their mates. Emotions will be high and kids will play to the support of their peers. You may lose face in front of the crowd and this will not do your credibility much good.

In a similar way to dealing with conflict between a student and a teacher, select your witnesses and then you can see both students separately. I would recommend you select a number of witnesses and also see them individually to avoid any chance of a mutually pre-arranged story. Remember you are after facts about what really happened. Also by seeing several witnesses it is harder for anyone to know who has 'grassed up' the fighters. Written statements will be necessary in serious brawls.

Both students will be upset, and the knack is to let them give their own account and show you are prepared to listen and understand what they are saying. You should tell them your wish is to remedy the disagreement and to find a way forward. Again, written statements will be necessary. Parents may want to see you about the event. After investigations are complete you may find that both parties will agree to disagree. There's nothing wrong with that as long as you stress the serious consequences of rekindling the hostilities.

In very serious assaults the police will need to be involved. Any injuries sustained by a victim of assault by a fellow pupil should be photographed on the school digital camera. I have found this helpful when the parents of the assailant attempt to challenge the school's disciplinary response. In the majority of cases, the kind of fracas you will encounter is easily sorted within the parameters of the school-discipline or behaviour policy. Do not recommend a temporary exclusion or place someone on behaviour report for a 'one off' minor skirmish.

It is all too easy for staff to refer any confrontational issues to the head of year when they could easily sort out the problem themselves. Sometimes all that is needed is a note in your tray about a petty duel and the fact that it was stopped and dealt with by the teacher. Staff have a tendency to revoke any responsibility for such an investigation. These minor feuds can often be sorted in minutes, but some try to leave it all to the year head.

Two young teachers were on their way back from the local pub at the end of lunchtime and came across two Year 7s pushing and shoving each other. They seemed as violent as a pair of eunuchs in Mothercare. The crowd had gathered and were goading them into drawing blood. Fortunately for the local blood bank the bout was stopped by our two NQTs and both pupils were brought to me.

'I've just broken up this fight with these two!' said one excitedly. 'It seemed like six of one and half a dozen of the other to me,' he continued.

'No it weren't, Sir!' said one of the microbial boxers who

seemed quite upset at the teacher's brief report. 'It was only me and him!' he explained. I spoke with our two new teaching recruits about how they should have responded, and also why they shouldn't breathe best bitter over everyone with a full afternoon's teaching ahead of them.

One of the schools where I spent around eight years of my teaching life was at a large comprehensive on an east end of London overspill estate. It was like being back in my native Salford. The area had many social problems. There was poverty and high rates of crime. Someone once was reported to have left their Rottweiler in a car while visiting a local shop, and when they came out the car was gone and the dog was up on bricks! A colleague of mine tried to convince me a recent town-twinning exercise had matched the area with a place called Scheissenhole in Germany.

I fall back on such memories because I had to face a most irate member of the public who came in to more than complain about the chronic misbehaviour of one of my Year 11 students. A terrified school receptionist summoned me to the foyer. There facing me was a huge lady who resembled Taras Bulba. Her arms were a gallery of tattoos and her hair appeared as wild as a South American rainforest. She was a woman of immense proportions with a bottom enough for seven. The lady was pacing the floor shouting expletives, while simultaneously wielding an aluminium clothes prop. She had a face that would instantly set a jelly.

In short, she had come in to complain about Frank Cheung of Year 11. Frank turned out to be a knicker bandit who would frequently remove ladies undergarments from the washing lines on the estate. This morning the growling lady in front of me had caught him in the act and fortunately for her (but unfortunately for me and Frank) she recognized his school tie. In a potentially troublesome situation like this, it is always best to try to remove the person from such a public place. I asked her to come to my office to discuss the nature of her complaint. She refused and still carried on shouting about castrating the culprit. I have précised and refined her vocabulary.

In a situation like this it's best to stand there and let them have their say. They have only so much adrenaline (testosterone in her case) and they will eventually burn themselves out. When it looks as though the tide is starting to recede, you can then start to explore the possibility of a conversation. It took her a good ten minutes to accept a sentence from me. I asked her to put down the clothes prop she was currently using as an assegai. Try to remain calm in a situation like this. Do not shout back. Listen to their story and promise you will take immediate action and that you will investigate the matter thoroughly. Do not let them have access to a pupil or pupils. In the case of Frank, she would have emasculated him. She said she wanted him prosecuted there and then.

The link between the theft and her presence at the school was Frank's school tie. To identify Frank was easy. He was the only very tall Chinese boy in Year 11. She confirmed his identity from our year mugshots. The bottom line of this incident was that it was theft and a crime that took place outside school. I said that I would telephone her later that day and asked her not to contact the police until I had spoken to Frank and his parents. Fortunately the woman agreed to this, which meant she could go home. There was no need to get the police and parents up the school for any interviews. In a situation like this, any questions the police may have for Frank could be asked at home in front of his parents.

This action also gave me time to speak with Frank who, when asked to empty his bag, produced 14 pairs of undies with a wide range of dimensions. He would also ask for 18 other acts of 'drawers theft' to be taken into consideration. School job done.

To summarize

1. Do not act in a reflex way, think things through calmly if you can.
2. Try to defuse and take the tension out of a situation.
3. Do not lose your temper.
4. Do not shout back at the person and appear to lose it!
5. Be careful of your body language, maintain personal space, do not eyeball anyone, etc.
6. Separate the two parties and allow them to calm down.
7. Never speak to them in front of an audience.
8. Interview them separately and find out the facts. Ask them to document their statements.
9. If it involves a member of the school staff, ask them to complete an incident report.
10. Offer both sides support and indicate you will give the matter your immediate attention.
11. Ask for witness statements in order to get an accurate and balanced account of the incident. Statements to be put in writing, dated and signed.
12. Collect and keep any other intelligence you may need.
13. Check on any previous altercations. Look for patterns.
14. Inform who needs to be told, e.g. head of department, headteacher, line manager, parents.
15. Document any actions or recommendations you take.
16. Deal with any disciplinary matters in accordance with the school policy on behaviour. Inform both parties of your action.
17. In serious cases of assault photograph physical injuries and insist upon medical attention. Be prepared for the police to get involved via parents.

18. Never let a parent or member of the public have access to pupils. Try to allow them to use photographs to identify students.
19. Offer strategies/solutions in cases of repeated confrontational behaviour by students and staff.
20. Did you collate all of that paperwork?

8 Special difficulties experienced by some of your students

If God had wanted a gerbil

If God had wanted a gerbil
He should have saved up like me
and gone to the pet shop and bought one
that's doing things 'properly'

If God had wanted a gerbil
then I think it's awfully mean
to have made me drop mine and kill it
when I fed it and kept it so clean

If God had wanted a gerbil
He should have taken its cage and its straw
No. I won't have another gerbil
Just in case God wants some more.

Unknown

Unless you have lost someone who was very close to you, it will be difficult for you to truly understand the emptiness, shock and numbness a person will feel when a bereavement occurs. I remember a tutor saying that he felt out of his depth when he heard that the father of one of his tutees had suddenly died. A youngster who tragically lost his mum commented that some of his teachers and friends really didn't know how to cope or what to say.

In your role as head of year you will have to deal with the issues relating to bereavement within the family of a member of your year group. The tutor team and the subject teachers of the student will often look to you for some help in enabling them to cope and know what to say and do.

One of the first duties is for you to make contact with the family. I find putting together a letter of condolence to both the parent and the student creates the first contact. In this letter, express your sympathy with their loss. You should then indicate that the school will offer to the family as much support and special consideration as they should need at this sad time. Mention that if there is anything the school can do then they should not hesitate to contact you or their child's tutor. Ask if it is acceptable for you or the tutor to inform the child's tutor group and friends. This initial communication will help later. Your next responsibility is to ensure that all members of staff know of the bereavement, including LSAs, office and ancillary staff, including the caretaker.

When you and the child's tutor have informed the members of the tutor group the two of you will probably face questions from them. Avoid giving too many details. Circumstances surrounding the death are really private matters. The job is then to prepare them for the return of the child. The tutor group should be a mutually supportive unit and want to pave the way for this return. The quality of the tutor often governs the degree of support that will be given at this time. You may have to substitute for an inept or clueless tutor but if this is the case, ask them to watch you and to learn from the way you handle the task. The group may be anxious about what to do and say. The child is likely to have a few close friends in the group. It is helpful to explore ways as to how they can be supportive. Some of the tutor group may want to respond by writing a letter to their friend. Give them the help they will require. Find out from the parents if it would be acceptable for flowers to be sent by the group. Some funerals prefer donations to be made, payable to research organizations, charity groups or hospitals. Some close friends may wish to attend the funeral. Again, seek permission from the home. A representative from the school staff should also seek approval to attend. The headteacher may want to do this. Often the head will feel it more appropriate for the tutor or year head to fulfil this role. I always feel it should be the member of staff who has the best working relationship with the student.

This preparation work tackled by you and the tutor will hopefully make the reintegration of the student back into school life a less difficult process. Many bereaved pupils are anxious to return to the normality of school life. It is wise to see the student in private and tell them the school is here to offer any help and support they may need. Say to them that if they need some moments to themselves, there is always somewhere for them to go. Suggest your office or somewhere similar. Avoid recommending the medical room, that is usually a place which is far from private with its incessant stream of pyrexia, nausea and dislocations.

You should work in association with the tutor in monitoring the progress of the child over the next few months. Some children's grief may lay dormant for some time. Some children do not appear to show any of the expected signs of grief. All children react differently during this traumatic period but their feelings will be no different to those experienced by adults. Some will express their grief as anger or feelings of guilt. Some will be aggressive or show signs of panic or anxiety. Some may withdraw and not wish to communicate their innermost thoughts.

Parents will want to be kept informed of any problems. There may be difficulties with concentration in lessons or incomplete homework. Allow some initial latitude here and hopefully the situation will improve. It is sometimes a difficult path to follow in terms of making special allowances for students and knowing for how long this should continue.

I would suggest that if you continue to have concerns about the child's well-being and you have discussed these worries with their parents, then the possibility of some help from professional services such as the GP or bereavement counsellor may be worth pursuing. The child's family should arrange this contact but you could suggest a letter outlining the school's concerns, which may be of help in speeding up the referral process.

There is one last suggestion I would make relating to bereavement. You and the tutor should be mindful of the special times when memories may return. These will include anniversaries, birthdays and Christmas, and may be occasions requiring extra vigilance and consideration.

There are sometimes instances when some member of the year group has a problem relating to sickness at home. It may be a parent, brother, sister or grandparent. Such changes to the normal daily routine will frequently bring about new pressures or responsibilities for all concerned. Youngsters may have to change sleeping arrangements. They may have to move out of their bedroom to allow Nan to move in. This room may have doubled as a place where homework was done. Hospital visits give parents new challenges and bring about alterations in domestic convention. Household chores that normally function at set times during the week may also be affected. There may be new demands placed on the children in the family. These can range from preparing the evening meal, taking and collecting younger family members to and from school, doing the shopping and washing clothes.

In short, the child may have new concerns and time-consuming pressures.

At school we may not have been informed of these changes. Parents may not have had the time or even forgotten to mention this to the tutor. Symptoms of such changes at home can sometimes manifest themselves in a sudden cessation in extra-curricular activities undertaken by the student. The child's homework may suffer. I have known children to fall asleep in lessons because of changes in their workload at home. Some youngsters may not be able to keep themselves clean, as laundry duties at home take place on an irregular basis.

Work with these families and try to make the child's daily school experience as uncomplicated as possible. Inform teachers so that clumsy or insensitive remarks can be avoided. It may mean that temporary allowances can be made regarding coursework or homework. Ask parents for updates in their circumstances. It shows that you and the school care and that the home–school experience is, indeed, a partnership. In certain circumstances both you and the parents may feel it helpful if some assistance is sought for the family through Education Welfare or Social Services.

In these situations, be aware that some students are reluctant to discuss these matters. This may be because of their dignity and pride. It could be that they feel the life they experience at home should be completely separate from school and should not demand attention. School can offer some degree of normality compared to their hectic and chaotic life at home. It is important to respect the student's wishes and never be too searching with the questions you ask the child. Create a positive climate by indicating you and the tutor are there to discuss any worries if they so wish.

Nearly half of all children in the UK will see their parents divorce. In 2001, 147,000 children under 16 saw their parents divorce, and just under a quarter of these were under the age of 5 (Office for National Statistics, Census 2001). These figures mean that in a year group there will be many students whose parents are separated and either divorced or in the process of seeking a divorce. Divorce and separation can produce similar feelings of loss in children to those in bereavement. Members of pastoral teams in particular should be mindful of the way kids can feel when a marriage breaks down. They will sometimes feel torn between two parents, angry with one or both of these parents for causing the separation. They may even blame themselves for the failure of the marriage. They may feel rejected and insecure, to the degree that some kids have even said they are worried they will be left on their own if both parents go it alone.

Family breakdown will create many problems that schools should understand and often be able to offer help. The majority of one-parent families consist of children residing with their mother. Such change in family circumstances will bring about financial problems and a sudden alteration in the domestic routine. Some lone parents with teenage children will struggle to cope with adolescent rebellion on top of the changes caused by separation. Some fathers may belittle Mum's efforts, in a subtle attempt to be seen as the favourite or charismatic parent. They may indulge their children in an attempt to ingratiate themselves. There will often be problems with the children if one or both parents decide to remarry. Common feelings of having to share Mum or Dad with somebody else add to the initial trauma of the divorce.

If problems surface that are rooted in such domestic change, you should always give your time and be prepared to listen to the student. It is essential you tackle a student's feelings rather than any behaviour that is causing concern. However, you will not be able to solve these often complex family problems but you will be able to offer support to these casualties of the family breakdown and often suggest professional agencies who may be of some help. Keep a careful eye on these students as they approach milestones in their lives. These will include impending public examinations, or the anniversary of when a parent walked out on the family.

Meetings with parents may not prove as straightforward as planned. If there is a problem with the child, be careful that the session is not used as a forum for apportioning blame. You should tread a neutral line and push for a cooperative approach in the best interest of the child's education. There is no place for you criticizing or patronizing any parent. Keep accurate notes of the meeting. In some access or custody cases the minutes may be required by a parent's legal representative. I was once contacted by the CSA (Child Support Agency), for information. They can be effective on occasions!

When you contact parents by letter, ensure it is correctly titled and addressed. Invitations to school activities, parents' evenings and copies of reports should go to the right people. Any errors in such a simple task may give ammunition to an aggrieved parent who will protest that the school and other parent are deliberately minimizing his/her role in their child's life.

On a final note, you should notify the office staff of access, injunctions and custody decisions. Occasionally parents without access rights will arrive at the school asking to see their child. If the staff at the school's reception have been given this information they will contact a senior member of staff to handle the matter.

One of the least pleasant elements of your job is dealing with issues involving child protection. A child is more likely to make a disclosure to an adult whom they feel they can talk to and trust. Very often this person is a tutor, a particular subject teacher or the head of year. Subject teachers are occasionally informed of an area of concern through written work. Children will make such initial contact because they want any abuse to stop. The abuse could be from someone they love. The intention, in this case, is to put a stop to the abuse but not to allow the perpetrator to be sent to prison.

All staff in the school should have received training in child-protection issues. They should be made aware of any of the indicators of possible physical, sexual and emotional abuse and neglect. They should be clear about the procedure for reporting these concerns to the designated person responsible for child protection. If such a disclosure is made to you as year head, your subsequent action should be no different to any other member of staff in the school. The child-protection policy protocol should be meticulously followed. It is essential that you listen to the child and allow them to recall freely what has happened. You must reassure the child that you will believe what they are telling you. However, should the child ask for total confidentiality in this matter, remember you cannot agree to this. Point out that the information must be passed on to people who can help with this matter. Your role is not to question or get statements from the child. However, as soon after the disclosure has been made you should make notes about the words used by the child in their disclosure. Sign, date and record the time of the conversation and immediately relay this information to the designated person responsible for child protection.

The school should make it clear in their child-protection policy that leading questions should not be asked and that no secrets are to be shared between the child and the adult to whom they are making the disclosure. I cannot emphasize enough how important it is to follow this prescribed procedure. I have encountered a number of instances when staff have exceeded their professional boundaries in child-protection cases and the school has received a reprimand for such malpractice. The important point to remember is that such a process is in place because the welfare of the child is paramount and that the young person needs protection from harm. Do ensure all of your tutor team are cognizant of such procedure. Concerns and observations about a child's welfare frequently come from them and they may be the teacher with whom the child is likely to share their anxieties and fears.

The person in the school with responsibility for child protection will often decide to notify parents before a referral is made. However, if contact cannot be made, this matter will still go ahead to the child-protection team (a social worker and a police officer trained in child-protection work). The only circumstances in which a parent will not be informed of a referral is if it is considered the child might be at a greater risk of harm as a result of this contact or such action may impede a criminal investigation.

The duty of the child-protection team will be to investigate the matter. On a practical note, this team can often take its time arriving at the school. I recall being threatened with a club hammer by an irate parent demanding to take their child home. We had some difficulty in stalling him until the team eventually assembled some two hours later.

Once more, record keeping is an essential skill in the job. You may be asked to work in close association with the designated person for child protection. Any documentation the school receives concerning a child-protection investigation or minutes of meetings relating to this, should be held securely and confidentially in accordance with the Data Protection Act. Similarly, any documented concerns from a member of staff relating to this investigation, should be kept safely and securely by the named teacher responsible for child protection. The school will usually have a pro forma which ensures notes are completed in the correct way, insisting on times, dates and outcomes of any meetings. Any person who completes these record sheets will need to ensure they distinguish between fact and opinion. These records can be required by a court of law. Any sharp lawyer will tear them apart if they appear as inaccurate, anaemic and full of opinions.

Many child-abuse cases never reach courts of law, but most require follow-up work and a monitoring period. Case conferences will usually be attended by a social worker allocated to the family, a member of the police child-protection team, an EWO and a representative from the school. The meeting will be chaired by a senior social worker or a senior Education Welfare Officer. Other parties such as the GP or school nurse will also be invited to attend. However, you will find that some will send their apologies and sometimes a written report. The head of year is frequently asked to represent the school and to provide a report on the child. This will provide information on progress in school, attendance, punctuality, behaviour and anything relating to the original child-protection inquiry.

It is sometimes difficult to prevent your personal feelings about a child-protection matter colouring your actions and reports. This is particularly so when you watch a child try to pick up the pieces of their lives because of abuse from an adult. You must maintain a professional approach to these matters even though you may wish to hand the abuser to the Cosa Nostra for retribution. In the course of your life as head of year you may have the misfortune to meet all of the forms of child abuse, some will sicken you and give you less faith in human nature. However, safeguarding the welfare of children and protecting them from harm is part of your job. Expect anything.

You may work in an English school in Caracas, a fee-paying, private school in the rolling hills of Devon, or an urban comprehensive in the city of Liverpool. Wherever you teach, bullying will happen. Dealing with bullying incidents will form part of your workload each year. All schools should now have in place an anti-bullying policy. Young people search for leadership, support and clarification from adults in the school. They expect this to be evident in the anti-bullying policy. When bullying is ignored or downplayed, pupils will suffer torment and harassment. The anti-bullying policy of the school should permeate through the PSHCE and the hidden curriculum of a school. Classroom teachers should be able to recognize signs of bullying and be able to respond effectively in accordance with this policy. Their aim is to produce safe classroom environments. The policy requires us all to sing from the same song sheet in the way we respond to instances of bullying.

The head of year is often perceived as being the master when it comes to dealing with victims and bullies. The year head is expected to have a strategy that always offers a solution to the problem. In reality, some instances of chronic bullying may result in unsatisfactory conclusions despite many hours being spent sorting out the concern. Do not be expected to solve everyone else's classroom problems. The classroom teacher and their head of department should not renege on their responsibilities. Year heads should insist that training is given to all staff in ways of dealing with bullying and this training should be revisited over a period of time.

When bullying is not simply confined to a classroom, then this is a time when you and the tutor will become involved. You will need to first attend to the victim and then deal with the bully. You will frequently discover that your victims have poor social skills, they are desperate to 'fit in' and lack confidence to seek help. They may blame themselves and believe they are being bullied because it is their own fault. The classmates of these victims sometimes find them unappealing and colourless. Whatever their characteristics, if a child approaches you for help or is referred to you because it is suspected they are being bullied, you must take immediate action.

You must approach the matter with care and sensitivity. Express relief that the matter is now out in the open and can be dealt with. You must allow the student to talk about the bullying. You must not allow your contact with the student to seem like an interrogation. Record what the student tells you about the problem and ask them for some information as to when and where these incidents took place. Year managers are good at looking for patterns. Ask the student to keep you informed of any future episodes.

In your meeting with the victim, do not focus on the shortcomings of the bully and do not over-react. Your job is to concentrate on what is the immediate problem and to offer them some practical and sensible advice. Inform the student you will thoroughly investigate the bullying and ask to see them at a future date. They should be asked to note any further examples and to report them to you. Tell the student that you must discuss this matter with their parents and inform them of the nature of the bullying and the course of action you will take.

When you attempt to resolve these difficulties be prepared to include reliable members of the peer group to provide support. Try to ensure the victim has access to a bully-free environment at all times. Suggest they avoid the known bully hot spots around the school. Suggest they change their route and times to and from school. Give the student a safe place to go if they feel vulnerable. Suggest places for the victim to go at break and lunchtimes that you know are supervised.

You must report the bullying to your line manager and also to your EWO. They too must be aware of the problem and the action you have taken or intend to take. Victims will experience terrifying periods of fear and anxiety. Some may even feel they cannot cope with things any more and fall into a sea of depression and despair. Should any child make any reference to wanting to end their life, you must take immediate action and obtain professional assistance.

If you discover the bullying is being perpetrated by a group of students, it is usual for there to be one or two individuals who are the nucleus of the problem. The rest will be hangers-on who seem to take courage from the herd. Trying to address the issue in such a case is more challenging, since you must clarify the role of each member of the crowd. Your bullies are often the attention seekers with a desire to establish a power base by taunting less-powerful members of the school. They believe they are popular and constantly remind the group of their power by committing such despicable acts. Collusion of their peers in the bullying process strengthens their perceived dominance, and the bullying will continue and worsen.

If the school climate is influenced by its anti-bullying policy, then undoubtedly it will be easier to discipline the wrongdoers. You must ensure the bullies see the effects of their anti-social behaviour. Support from responsible members of the year group can help. Bullying is wrong and must be punished in whatever way the school feels is acceptable. Parents must be informed about the chain of events and you must ask for their support in whatever the school wishes to do. A number of parents refuse to accept the degree of involvement of their child and cite bullying episodes involving other children about which you have no information. Be intransigent in these cases and keep to the facts. Make it more difficult for the bully to operate. This may mean keeping them apart from their peers for a period of time. Bullies dislike this, since many draw energy from their friendship group.

Just because your intervention may appear to have eased the situation, you must not strike the problem from your ever-increasing list of jobs. Continue to work with the tutor to monitor the progress made.

To summarize

Bereavement issues

1. Write a letter of condolence to the family.
2. Inform all staff in the school.
3. Do not give children too many details.
4. Prepare the tutor group for the child's reintegration.

5. Talk to the child's close friends about any support they can offer.
6. Find out the funeral arrangements.
7. See if the family will allow close friends to attend/send flowers.
8. A representative from the school staff should attend.
9. See the child in private on their return.
10. Tell them the school will try to help them through this sad time, e.g. if things get too much . . .
11. Monitor the progress of the child and keep parents informed.
12. Look for signs of grief which may surface after the reintegration period.
13. Note the important times such as Christmas, birthdays and other anniversaries.

Sickness at home

1. Make contact with the home as soon as you become aware of these circumstances.
2. Inform parents and the child of any temporary arrangements you have put in place to allow them to stay buoyant with their work.
3. Inform all staff of the circumstances.
4. Do EWS or Social Services need to assist family? Check with parents.
5. Respect any privacy the student may want, particularly when the family member has a psychiatric illness. Do not probe too deeply.

Family breakdown

1. When you are informed of the nature of the problem, see the student but be sensitive to their fragile state.

2. Tackle the feelings of the student rather than any sudden changes in their moods or behaviour.
3. Know your professional boundaries.
4. Offer to the parents the opportunity of support from professional agencies they may need, e.g. EWS, Social Services . . .
5. Do not take sides with or patronize either parent. Tread a neutral path.
6. Monitor the attendance, academic progress and demeanour of the child.
7. Keep accurate documented notes of any telephone calls, meetings, action plans that have taken place with both parents.
8. Inform administrative staff of any changes in circumstances so that any information from the school will be sent to the right people at the correct addresses.
9. Inform school reception staff of access arrangements and any potential problems. Note changes in custody post decree absolute.

Child-protection issues

1. Ensure all staff have read the school child–protection policy and know the prescribed procedures.
2. Staff should know who is the designated teacher responsible for child protection.
3. Always, always follow the protocol in child–protection matters.
4. Keep records of the progress of child–protection cases in a separate locked file in accordance with the Data Protection Act.
5. Be prepared to represent the school at case conferences and to report on the academic progress, behaviour and attendance of the child. You will also be asked to report on any other relevant problems.

6.   Be prepared to be called to attend in a court of law, should the need arise.

Bullying issues

1. Ensure all staff have read the school's anti-bullying policy, and are aware of the signs of bullying and how to respond.
2. Take prompt action and do not sideline bullying issues.
3. Talk and listen to the victim.
4. Look for any patterns.
5. Inform the victim's parents and tell them the action you will take.
6. Suggest strategies to the child that will lead to a reduction in the bullying.
7. Enlist peer-group support for the victim.
8. Ask for further episodes to be brought to your attention.
9. Mention a safe place for the child to go in times of crisis.
10. Deal with the bully and put in place any school discipline procedure.
11. Inform parents of bully.
12. Keep all of your paperwork, including witness statements, telephone calls to and from parents, dates, times, etc.

9 Common pastoral problems

Theft

The school office telephones you to assist a young member of staff to investigate the loss of a £20 note. This has been taken from the blazer pocket of a youngster in your year in the course of a science lesson. The student has brought the money in to school so that he can buy a CD on his way home.

When you arrive at the room, ask the teacher to explain to you how and when the theft was discovered. Your questions should take place in the classroom but out of earshot of the class. Did anyone leave the room during the lesson? Did the teacher go out of the room, leaving the class with no supervision? Have any items, money or possessions gone missing in previous lessons? Are there any patterns? Is there anything you should know that might have bearings on this incident? Ask to see the student outside the room and ask them similar questions. Did anyone know of this sum of money? Is the student certain that the money went missing in the lesson? When was the student last aware of the note being on his person? Has the student any suspicions as to whom may be responsible? Make certain the classroom teacher remains with the group while you are seeing the student. Do you, as head of year, have any ideas whom may be responsible? Are there any known thieves in the group?

Some thoughts on the problem:

1. How many students will have a £20 note on their person? If you find any, how can you prove the note is theirs? Maybe telephone a parent to see if they brought that kind of money into school today.

2. You cannot search a pupil. You can, however, ask them to turn out their pockets and bags. This is a time-consuming process, so enlist the help of the teacher. However, keep an eye on the rest of the group as you are doing this. Does anyone try to go into their pockets or bags before they are approached? Does anyone attempt to drop something on the floor or behind a radiator? Girls are often embarrassed about tampons and towels in their bags so the help of a female may make the inquiry more dignified. Ask them to show you the empty pockets. Some boys put notes like this in their sock. If needed, ask them to roll down their socks. If it has been put into their underwear then you have no chance! Notes easily slip into exercise books or textbooks. Purses, wallets and pencil cases need scrutiny.

3. Were students able to wander around the room during the lesson?

4. Where was the blazer during the lesson? Some students take them off and leave them some distance from where they were sitting.

5. Did any students leave the room during the course of the lesson? If this is the case then they could have taken it from the room. Check student's locker. There are often other places in the school where stolen items can easily be stashed. If no one left the room, then the money is still there.

6. If all of these attempts fail, give the students a blank piece of paper and ask them to write down anything they may know about the incident. Tell them not to sign it. You are after a clue and some pupils may be more likely to give you information if they can remain anonymous. It is often easy to identify handwriting at a later time. Make sure you stress the incident is a theft and may involve the police. Try to appeal to their better nature. Emphasize that such an act is both despicable and unpleasant and has happened to one of their classmates. Someone in our midst cannot be trusted and such an act makes us all feel uneasy and insecure. You may be lucky with a name! If you are given a name or names, see each student outside the classroom. Do not let the rest of the class leave until you have seen the student.

7. As soon as you allow them to leave the classroom and the thief is not identified then you can say cheerio to retrieving the money.

8. You will need to contact the child's parents to inform them of the theft. Explain what you have done and make clear that the school office is able to look after large sums of money for the student. Investigating this incident has taken much of your time.

9. Why wasn't the head of department called to deal with the matter?

10. In cases of theft you may often be able to use bluff to confirm the identity of a thief. You may know very little, but by giving the suspect an idea that you know plenty, is sometimes a detective practice that may prove helpful.

11. A word of caution about investigating thefts from a PE changing room. It is the PE teacher's responsibility to see students out of the changing room and then to lock up. They are then to let students back into this

room and supervise them until they leave. Far too frequently these rooms are left unlocked. This invites trouble. Money, watches and other items of value may not have been collected by the teacher. Free access is allowed to this area. Insist that the correct procedure is maintained. All heads of year will spend hours investigating thefts which could easily have been prevented by following such precautionary measures.

12. CCTV footage is a helpful technology of use in detecting thefts. The images also give you dates and times. My last school had some installed of rather dubious quality. The contrast and detail was so poor that everyone looked Afro-Caribbean. The video technology however, did prove particularly useful to me when I needed to arrest a rash of purse thefts. We apprehended the girl by setting up a situation that proved too tempting for her. You can also use bluff, by telling the kids the school has had micro cameras placed around the school. Stress, the cameras are so tiny, they could be anywhere!

13. Best of luck and remember the code of the Canadian Mountie, 'We always get our man!'

Self-harm

A girl in your year group tells you she has discovered that one of her friends is injuring herself. The girl wears wrist bands to mask the cuts and scars. Her friend is worried about her because she shows no intention of stopping the self-injury. The girl is asking you for help but is concerned that her friendship with the student will be put at risk.

Reassure the girl that she has done the right thing by alerting a teacher. Remember, she has approached you because she feels you are the best person to get help for her friend. Make notes on everything the girl tells you and thank her for discussing the problem. Say you will see the girl and try to get her the help she needs. Tell the friend you will try to protect her anonymity if you can, but you cannot lie to the girl. She will need to trust and feel comfortable with you when you discuss her troubles. You may introduce the session by commenting on the fact that several people have noticed her starting to wear these wrist bands and take it from there.

Self-injury is a complex and serious issue to deal with. Self-harm is often a coping mechanism for dealing with stressful experiences. It may be triggered by problems at home or at school. The student can have a very poor self-image. Self-harm is always a sign of something seriously being wrong with their life. This self-injury behaviour is a mechanism for dealing with the anger and despair they sometimes feel. Some people have feelings of guilt or shame and punish themselves by inflicting these injuries on themselves. It can sometimes be a way of coping with trauma.

You must act on this information and ask to see the girl. Make sure you set aside enough time for the conversation. This matter needs your full attention.

1. It is important to remember your professional boundaries here. You should act as a catalyst for the special help and counselling the girl may need. You are not a psychiatrist and you must never say you will keep your discussion a secret.
2. You can help by listening to the girl and take seriously any worries or problems she has. Show that you understand what she says, even if you are shocked by what she tells you.
3. Stay calm and remain in control of your feelings.
4. Tell the girl that it is possible to sort out the problems and suggest a way forward.

5. If the problems are peer-group based then suggest ways of making the situation better.

6. If problems stem from the home then you can provide the breakthrough the child needs by addressing the concerns with the parents.

7. Whatever the case, the parents need to be aware of your discussion with the girl. Treatment often involves both individual and family work. You can help facilitate any family counselling the family may need via Education Welfare, the GP or the local health authority.

8. Make sure the girl gets the right kind of help as soon as possible.

9. Discuss the matter with the teacher in charge of child protection if you feel this is necessary. Inform your line manager and EWO.

10. The central issue is that the student has someone they can talk to and get support whenever they need it.

11. Self-harm is always a sign that something is seriously wrong, and you should never ignore any threats the student may make about ending their life.

Drugs in school

A Year 9 girl comes to tell you that both she and her friend have just been approached by a group of boys in your year and asked if they wanted to buy some drugs. The girls say that they were shown something in tin foil that looked like a small Oxo cube and the boys said it was cannabis.

Schools today should have in place a policy that specifically deals with drugs issues in the school. Within this structure there will be a protocol for dealing with incidents of this kind. Your duty is to work within the framework of this document in the way you investigate this episode. If you stray from such agreed procedures then any future success in completing the investigation to the school's satisfaction may be put in jeopardy.

You will need to act swiftly in this case while the supposed drugs are still on the school premises. The following suggestions may be of help to you in proceeding with this matter:

1. The 'drug' may be an Oxo cube, and the boys were playing around. Nevertheless you must handle the inquiry as though it is for real.
2. Ask both girls for a description of the boys. Show them photographs from your 'Rogue's Gallery'. Ask them to identify the pupil who offered them the drug and had the drug in his possession. What was the role of the rest of the boys in the group? Find out when and where this took place.
3. Ask both girls to write a statement of what took place. Place the girls in separate areas where they can complete their accounts. This is so that they cannot be seen to agree upon a story. This is important for any future enquiry as to how the incident was investigated. Ask them to date and sign these statements.
4. Inform the headteacher of the circumstances and tell him/her of your proposed actions.
5. Discover where the boys are now. If they are still together, ask a reliable member of staff to sit with them and keep a careful eye on anything they may try to do. One of them may have the drugs and will attempt to discard them. They are to sit in silence under that teacher's supervision while you see them individually. This is to avoid the possibility of any story being agreed upon by the boys. You must rule out any possibility of collusion. If you have the personnel to allow you to keep the boys separate, then even better. A boy who wants to visit the toilet must be

accompanied by another teacher. Again, it is possible he wishes to dispose of the drugs.

6. Interview each student separately and ask them to turn out their pockets and bag. You cannot search them but ask them to remove their blazers and give them to you. If you have apprehended them early enough then you should discover the package. Remember socks!

7. Take separate statements from all the boys. Again, they should write their statements in isolation from the others to avoid concocting a story. They are to date and sign these statements.

8. Stress the serious nature of the incident and the future involvement of the police. They may wish to treat this affair as possession with intent to supply.

9. Ascertain each boy's involvement with the drug. Determine who brought the drug into school and from whom it was purchased.

10. Inform the headteacher of your findings. Inform parents of the students as to their son's individual role in this incident.

11. The main points of concern are that drugs have been brought onto the school premises and also that these drugs were offered for sale to other students. The disciplinary code within the school's drugs policy should prescribe the sanctions the school may consider.

A cautionary note about statements from students:

When you take a statement from a student, explain to them that you need something put in writing so that neither of you forgets anything they have told you. Allow them to write their statement on their own so that you cannot be accused of influencing their words. Instruct the student to include everything they have told you. Read through their statement after they have finished, and see if there are any essential pieces of information missing from the account. Remind the student that this needs to be an honest and accurate representation of what they have just told you. Highlight any information they have given you that has been omitted and ask them to include such facts.

A special non-attendance issue: school refusal

The non-attendance problems you will usually face are from pupils who cite issues such as boredom, problems with teachers, inappropriate curriculum, bullying, peer-group pressure and fear of returning to school and getting into trouble. There are, however, a small percentage of children who experience an anxiety disorder, giving them an irrational and persistent fear of going to school. These children are said to be suffering from school phobia, or school refusal. Children who are school phobic show behaviour different to a truanting student. They usually want to be close to their parents or carer, whereas truants do not.

A boy in your year has attendance figures that recently have been causing you concern. Matters have deteriorated now and the boy is refusing to come to school. Your preliminary enquiries with the boy's parents as to the drop in his attendance, revealed he was suffering from stomachaches and headaches. In short, he claimed he was too unwell to attend school.

1. You will already have discussed your concerns about the boy's recent poor attendance with the EWO. Parents will also have received telephone calls and letters of enquiry from you concerning their child's patchy attendance.

2. Education Welfare may be in the process of insisting upon medical certification when suddenly the concern changes into school refusal.

3. It is now essential to meet with the child and his parents to determine the exact nature of the school avoidance.

4. Some reasons for school refusal may be home related. These could include parents recently divorcing, a recent bereavement, chronic sickness in the family, financial problems or moving house.

5. School issues could precipitate the non-attendance. These may include threats of physical harm by a bully, existing learning difficulties, poor athletic ability, teasing about their appearance or perceptions that teachers will criticize or ridicule their work. I have known some school-phobic students fear they will faint or be sick in school assemblies. One student had worries about using school toilets.

6. Whatever the problem turns out to be, it is important that both you and the parents recognize the issue and work in partnership to alleviate the difficulties. Once the underlying cause is understood then a customized package can be put together to help the child.

7. The programme could involve the student attending school on certain days. Try phasing the student back into school in half-day blocks. The aim is to allow them to slowly teethe their way back into school life.

8. It is worth trying adjustments in work assignments if the student is concerned about confidence in their academic abilities.

9. In the early days, you may have to make certain concessions relating to the school day.

10. You may have to organize special toileting arrangements.

11. Act quickly if the refusal involves bullying.

12. Inform staff of these special concessions and ask for their support in whatever blueprint you feel may help.
13. Try to get the youngster to participate in activities they enjoy, to make school a happier place.

Whatever formula you choose for the child, the aim is to have the child return to school and to attend lessons. This cooperative approach, which includes the support and encouragement the student needs, may take some time to fully return the child back into school life. If school phobia is extreme and is not tackled early enough, then support and professional advice from a child-guidance counsellor or psychiatrist may be the next way forward.

Insensitive conduct from a colleague

There are times when staff will disappoint you. Instances of such disillusion may include failing to complete duties central to their job descriptions or by allowing a disciplinary incident to sour because of poor behaviour management. There will be occasions, too, when you seriously question why some teachers took the Queen's shilling (nowadays, anything up to £5,000 if you teach physics) and sign up for the profession. You, as head of year, may have to pick up the pieces of their unprofessional and sometimes insensitive behaviour involving the students in your care.

A physical education teaching colleague sends you a note about a boy in your Year 7 who is refusing to shower after PE lessons. The teacher wants to bring the boy's parents in to school to focus on health and hygiene issues. He also wants you to discipline the boy for disobedience. The boy truanted from the lesson last week and was found in the toilets during the lesson.

The boy concerned has undescending testicles and this information is clearly mentioned in the year medical records. He is usually a pleasant and well-behaved boy who is making good progress.

1. The teacher's reflex behaviour could cause very serious consequences, particularly if parents do challenge his actions. They may be tempted to describe the teacher's behaviour as bullying, insensitive and extremely unprofessional. You too will share similar thoughts. You must act swiftly to prevent even more damage being done by this colleague.

2. You suspect the reason for the refusal to shower concerns the boy's medical condition. The teacher has clearly failed to consult the medical information on students. This dossier is continuously updated and is an important read for all subject teachers. If the teacher is aware of the boy's condition and maintains his intransigent response, then he certainly needs a reprimand about his indifference and unsympathetic perspective. There is no place in schools for anyone who has trained at the Pol Pot school of education.

3. Prevent the teacher from contacting home. Tell him you will speak with him after you've had a chance to do some research. Ask him to write down exactly what happened.

4. See the student. Ask the student to describe his feelings that led to his reluctance to shower and to truant. Again, concentrate on the student's sentiments rather than the behaviour. Find out exactly what the teacher said and did. Were there any witnesses? See witnesses and obtain statements. How many times has it happened? Ask the student to write his own statement.

5. Has the boy discussed the matter with his parents? If so,

you will need to complete your research as quickly as possible.

6. Tell the boy you will sort out the problem with the teacher and that he should not continue to worry. You are there to help.

7. Read through all the statements and then consult the teacher. Point out to him that all of this unpleasantness could have been avoided if he had perused the medical data.

8. Point out that before any contact home is made, it is wise to contact the tutor or head of year. In this case it seemed a fait accompli, the teacher was going to contact home. All he wanted the head of year to do, in this case, was to reinforce the discipline.

9. Hopefully, the teacher will see the complete picture. He may still be concerned about the student showering after the lesson. Can a compromise be reached here? Can the student be subtly and inconspicuously allowed to shower first or last?

10. See the student and outline what you have done. Is he happy with the new arrangements? Arrange to see the student for a chat in a couple of weeks' time.

11. The teacher should apologize to the student for the unhappiness he has caused.

12. Contact the parents and settle any of their concerns.

13. Mention the matter to the teacher's head of department and your line manager. The boy's tutor will also need to know. Ask them to monitor the boy's progress.

10 Some final words

I spent some of the most enjoyable years of my teaching life as a head of year. You find you really earn your weekends. Do not be tempted to take on too much. Do not be afraid to say 'no' to people, particularly when they are asking you to do something that is their responsibility. Try to keep organized by having a diary and a 'things to do' sheet. You will soon acquire the skills necessary to prioritize items that need attention.

Always take time to think a problem through. Think of all possible outcomes of any action you do or do not choose to take. I have known some year managers flounder because they did not give enough thought to a problem. A matter brought to their attention on a Friday which they deemed could wait until Monday, sadly deteriorates over the weekend. This is particularly important if it embraces any potential child-welfare issues. Yes, try to think ahead and ask yourself, 'What could happen if . . . ?'

Try to socialize despite having a heavy caseload and teaching commitment. Learn to pace yourself and do not take too much work home with you at evenings and weekends. It is also amazing how far you will walk around the school building in a week, simply doing your job!

Show a willingness to develop your professional skills and try to attend the courses that are right for you. NAPCE (the National Association for Pastoral Care in Education) is a professional pastoral body based at the University of Warwick. Your school should be a member. If it is not, then ask your headteacher to subscribe. They organize national and local courses designed to focus on pastoral issues. It is good to be able to chat with fellow year heads and to discuss common issues.

It is wise to remember that your colleagues may not always tick at your pace. I worked with one head of department who was full of assurances but very little action. We referred to her as the Turkish Delight girl. She was from Peterborough and was full of eastern promise.

If there is one thing I will say about the job, it is to expect the unexpected. Who knows what your day will bring for your attention?

The job however, implores you to possess a sense of humour. It is the kids in school that keep you young. Some of the things they do and say will make you smile.

I was supporting a supply teacher who was in the process of registering a lively tutor group. She was calling the names of the students and I was just about to leave her to it, when she came to Ramana Elthorpe in the registration procedure. Ramana was a doleful girl, built like the European butter mountain. The lady paused and enquired, 'Ramana? You don't hear that name everyday!'

'Well, I do!' growled Ramana.

My final encounter with student mirth was at an inter-form basketball competition in the last week of school. It was organized by a loud, no-nonsense, head of PE. He did not need a megaphone to deliver instructions. He was the human equivalent of a sonic boom. The teams had been assigned the letters A, B . . . and so on. At the end of each match he would bellow directions to the groups. One of the teams contained a rather anaemic character named Daljeet Patel. He was a pleasant lad but poor young Daljeet didn't have much going for him. He had all the future of a snowman. One of Daljeet's many problems was being slow at making sense of information. The rapid orders from our stentorian head of PE echoed through the sports hall.

'Right! I want A on, C off, G on and F off!' he cried. The rather confused Daljeet, questioned the human foghorn.

'Who was that, Sir?' he enquired.

'I said F off, Daljeet!' roared the impatient decibel man.

'There's no need to be like that, Sir!' replied a wounded Daljeet.

I wish you every success in your new job. But remember two things. Keep all your paperwork intact and expect anything!

A head of year's reading list

Assemblies

Mullen, P. (1979), *Assembling*. London: Edward Arnold

Bullying

Elliott, M. (2002), *Bullying: Practical Guide to Coping for Schools*. London: Pearson.

Tattum, D. and Lane, D. (1989), *Bullying in Schools*. London: Trentham Books.

Child anxiety, abuse, family breakdown

Atkinson, M. and Hornby, G. (2002), *A Mental Health Handbook for Schools*. London: Routledge UK.

Child protection

NSPCC Publications (2005), *Worried? Need to Talk?* An information pack for teachers.

Whitney, B. (2004), *Protecting Children – A Handbook for Teachers and School Managers*. London: Routledge Falmer.

Conflict

Katz, N. and Lawyer, T. (1994), *Preventing and Managing Conflict in Schools*. Thousand Oaks, California: Corwin Press.

Drugs in schools

DfES paper 0092 2004 (2004), *Drugs: Guidance for Schools*. London: DfES.
McFadyean, M. (1997), *Drugs Wise*. London: Icon Books.

Managing people

Bush, T. and Middlewood, D. (eds) (1997), *Managing People in Education*. London: Paul Chapman Publishing.

NAPCE staff development resources

Sharp, S. (1997), *Reducing School Bullying. What works?*
Wagner, P. (1992), *Developing Effective Links with Parents.*
Wagner, P. (1993), *Children and Bereavement, Death and Loss.*
Watkins, C., Carnell, E., Lodge, C., Wagner, P. (1998), *Learning about Learning.*
Watkins, C. (1998), *Improving School Behaviour.*
Watkins, C. (1992), *Whole School PSE Policy and Practice.*

Parents

Kirby, M. (1995), *Working with Parents. A Quick Guide.* London: Daniels Publishing.

School refusal

Heyne, D. and Rollings, S. (2002), *School Refusal*. London: Blackwell.

Self-harm

Plevoets, A. (2002), *By Their Own Hand*. London: Jessica Kingsley Publishing.
Self Harm Support Organisation Free Booklet (2005), *The Truth About Self Harm*. www.selfharmuk.org.uk.

Special educational needs

Chivers, M. (2005), *Dyslexia and Other Learning Difficulties – A Parent's Guide*. Peterborough: Forward Press.

Teaching and learning

Carnell, E. and Lodge, C. (2002), *Supporting Effective Learning*. London: Paul Chapman Publishing.

Truancy

Reid, K. (2002), *Truancy: short and long term solutions*. London: Routledge Falmer.

NAPCE (National Association for Pastoral Care in Education)
Institute of Education
University of Warwick
Coventry CV4 7AL
Tel 024765 23810
napce@napce.org.uk

Index